# SERMON
# OUTLI
### ON
# PRA

GW00599588

**Books by Al Bryant:**

*Climbing the Heights*
*Day by Day with C. H. Spurgeon*
*Revival Sermon Outlines*
*Sermon Outlines for Evangelistic Occasions*
*Sermon Outlines on Bible Characters (Old Testament)*
*Sermon Outlines on Bible Characters (New Testament)*
*Sermon Outlines on the Deeper Life*
*Sermon Outlines on Prayer*
*Sermon Outlines for Special Occasions*
*Sermon Outlines for Worship Services*

# SERMON
# OUTLINES
## ON
# PRAYER

compiled by
## Al Bryant

**KREGEL PUBLICATIONS**
Grand Rapids, Michigan 49501

Cover and book design: Alan G. Hartman

**Library of Congress Cataloging-in-Publication Data**

Sermon outlines on Prayer / compiled and edited by Al
Bryant.

p. cm.
Includes index.
1. Prayer—Sermons—Outlines, syllabi, etc. I. Bryant,
Al, 1926-       .

| BV213.S47 | 1992 | 251'.01—dc20 | 91-39390 |
| | | | CIP |

ISBN 0-8254-2194-2

1 2 3 4 5 Printing/Year 96 95 94 93 92

Printed in the United States of America

# CONTENTS

*Foreword* . . . . . . . . . . . . . . . .6
*Textual Index* . . . . . . . . . . . . .7
An Alphabet of Personal
   Prayers . . . . . . . . . . . . . . . .9
A Prayer-Meeting in
   Apostolic Times . . . . . . . .10
Asking . . . . . . . . . . . . . . . . . .11
Boldness at the Throne . . . .12
The Believer's Prayer . . . . . .14
Characteristics of Prayer in
   James 5 . . . . . . . . . . . . . .15
Christ's Prayer in
   Gethsemane . . . . . . . . . . .15
Effectual Fervent Prayer . . .16
Hindrances to Prayer . . . . . .17
The Hypocrite's Prayer . . . . .18
In Order That Our Prayers
   May Be Answered . . . . . .19
Importunity in Prayer in the
   Life of Jesus . . . . . . . . . . .20
Jacob's Prayer . . . . . . . . . . .23
Nehemiah's Prayer . . . . . . . .24
Persistent Prayer . . . . . . . . .26
Paul's Prayer for the
   Philippians . . . . . . . . . . . .27
Petition . . . . . . . . . . . . . . . .28
Power in Prayer . . . . . . . . . .31
Prayer . . . . . . . . . . . . . . . . .32
Prayer: An Attitude . . . . . . . .33
Prayer and Promise . . . . . . .33
Prayer . . . . . . . . . . . . . . . . .33
Prayer Encouraged . . . . . . . .34
Prayer for the Church . . . . .36
Prayer Found in the Heart . .38
The Prayer God Will Not
   Despise . . . . . . . . . . . . . .40
Prayer: Its Oughtness . . . . . .42
Prayer: Its Privilege and
   Power . . . . . . . . . . . . . . . .43
Prayer: Jacob Wrestling
   with the Angel . . . . . . . . .44
Prayer of Faith . . . . . . . . . . .46
Prayer: Richard Baxter's
   Testimony . . . . . . . . . . . .47
The Prayer of the Penitent . .48
A Prayer Suited to All . . . . . .49
Prayer: The Greatest
   Ministry of All . . . . . . . . .51
Prayer: Three Kinds . . . . . . .52
Prayer of Faith . . . . . . . . . . .53
Prevailing Prayer . . . . . . . . .54
Seven Facts About Prayer . .55
Principles of Prayer . . . . . . .56
The Secret of Successful
   Prayer . . . . . . . . . . . . . . .58
How Should We Pray? . . . . .59
A Study of Prayer . . . . . . . . .60
Unavailing Prayer . . . . . . . . .63
Prayer Promises . . . . . . . . . .64

# FOREWORD

Martin Luther once said, "As a shoemaker makes a shoe, and a tailor makes a coat, so ought a Christian to pray. Prayer is the daily business of a Christian." Prayer is to be an integral part of the Christian's daily life, as it was in the lives of such Old and New Testament characters as Abraham, Moses, Peter and Paul. The outlines in this collection deal with prayer as intercession, as pleas for help on the part of a person or a group. Sometimes, prayer is secret, sometimes it is public. And sometimes it is "family" or "social" in focus. Many of the Psalms, for instance, are prayers presenting the petitions of a people or an individual. Someone has said, "Prayer is like the dove that Noah sent out of the ark. It blessed him not only when it returned with an olive branch in its mouth, but even when it never returned at all."

John Bunyan once wrote: "When thou prayest, rather let thy heart be without words than thy words without heart." This collection includes sermon outlines based on great Scripture texts concerning prayer, outlines based on prayer in the lives of Bible characters and outlines based on great Bible prayers themselves.

They are taken from both the Old and New Testament and include both topical and textual treatments.

It is the prayer of the compiler that they will enhance and enrich the spiritual lives of reader and hearer alike as they are presented from pulpits everywhere.

AL BRYANT

# TEXTUAL INDEX

## Genesis

18 . . . . . . . . . .62
22 . . . . . . . . . .23
22:9 . . . . . . . . .23
22:9, 12 . . . . . .23
22:10 . . . . . . . .23
22:11 . . . . . . . .23
24:63 . . . . . . . .54
27:34 . . . . . .9, 45
32 . . . . . . . . . .54
32:3 . . . . . . . . .44
32:6 . . . . . . . . .44
32:7 . . . . . . . . .44
32:9 . . . . .44, 54
32:9-12 . . . . . . .44
32:10 . . . . . . . .54
32:11 . . . . . . . .54
32:23 . . . . . . . .45
32:24 . . . . .17, 54
32:24,25ff . . . . .44
32:26 . . . . .17, 55
32:28 . . . . . . . .45
32:28-30 . . . . . .55

## Leviticus

16 . . . . . . . . . .52
21:8 . . . . . . . . .23

## Numbers

16:6 . . . . . . . . .17

## Exodus

3, 4 . . . . . . . . .62
11:14 . . . . . . . .17
32:10 . . . . . . . .17

## 1 Samuel

1:13 . . . . . . . . .55
2:9 . . . . . . . . . .33
8:18 . . . . . . . . .61
16:7 . . . . . . . . .17

## 2 Samuel

7:27 . . . . . . . . .38
22 . . . . . . . . . .62

## 1 Kings

8 . . . . . . . . . . .62
8:59 . . . . . . . . .54

18:24 . . . . . . . .32
18:42 . . . . . . . .55

## 2 Kings

20:1-7 . . . . . . . .32

## 2 Chronicles

7:14 . . . . . . . . .59
20:4 . . . . . . . . .11
32:20-22 . . . . . .32

## Nehemiah

1:1-11 . . . . . . . .24
2:2 . . . . . . . . . .55
4:4-6 . . . . . . . . .32
4:9 . . . . . . .14, 53
6:9 . . . . . . . . . .14
11:17 . . . . . . . .43

## Job

13:4 . . . . . . . . .38
23:3-8 . . . . . . . .63
27:10 . . . . . . . .18
30:20 . . . . . . . .17
42:8 . . . . . . . . .17

## Psalms

4:2 . . . . . . . . . .38
9:12 . . . . . . . . .59
10:17 . . . . . . . .59
16:1 . . . . . . . . .9
17:8 . . . . . . . . .9
25:18 . . . . . . . .9
25:21 . . . . . . . .9
26:2 . . . . . . . . .9
26:11 . . . . . . . .9
27:11 . . . . . . . .9
27:14 . . . . .17, 33
31:3 . . . . . . .9, 33
31:15 . . . . . . . .9
32:8 . . . . . . . . .33
37:3 . . . . . . . . .33
37:4 . . . . . .33, 59
37:7 . . . . . . . . .33
40:1 . . . . . . . . .17
49:15 . . . . . . . .33
51:1,2 . . . . . . . .48
51:2 . . . . . . . . .33

51:10 . . . . . . . .14
54:1 . . . . . . . . .9
62:1 . . . . . . . . .33
62:5 . . . . . . . . .33
66:18 . . . .17, 58
67:6 . . . . . . . . .38
67:8 . . . . . . . . .33
71:1 . . . . . . . . .9
79:8 . . . . . . . . .49
86:11 . . . . . . . .9
89:7 . . . . . . . . .59
91 . . . . . . . . . .33
100:17 . . . . . . .40
106:4 . . . . . . . .9
107:6, 13, 19, 28 14
119:18 . . . . . . .9
119:25 . . . . . . .9
119:35 . . . . . . .9
119:77 . . . . . . .9
119:154 . . . . . .14
138:6 . . . . . . . .17
139:24 . . . . . . .9
141:3 . . . . . . . .9
145:18 . . . . . . .58

## Proverbs

1:23 . . . . . . . . .40
1:28 . . . . . . . . .63
15:8 . . . . . . . . .58
15:29 . . . . . . . .58

## Isaiah

1:4-15 . . . . . . . .63
6:7 . . . . . . . . . .46
7:10, 12 . . . . . .19
26:9 . . . . . . . . .59
55:6 . . . . . . . . .59
57:15 . . . . . . . .59
58:3-14 . . . . . .17
58:9 . . . . . . . . .59
59:1,2 . . . . . . . .17
63:7—64:12 . . .62
65:24 . . . . . . . .59

## Jeremiah

11:10-11 . . . . . .63
29:13 . . . . . . . .59
32:16 . . . . . . . .34
33:3 . . . . . . . . .34

## Lamentations

1:1-4 . . . . . . . . .63
2:10,11 . . . . . . .63
3:1-8 . . . . . . . . .63
3:22, 33ff . . . . .63
3:44 . . . . . . . . .63

## Ezekiel

8:17 . . . . . . . . .63

## Daniel

8:16 . . . . . . . . .54
8:27 . . . . . . . . .55
9:3-20 . . . . . . . .46
9:4-11 . . . . . . . .25
9:17 . . . . . . . . .36
9:21 . . . . . . . . .43
9:23 . . . . . . . . .17
10:10 . . . . . . . .17

## Hosea

5:15 . . . . . . . . .19
7:11 . . . . . . . . .38
12:4 . . . . . . . . .54
12:4,5 . . . . . . . .45
12:4-6 . . . . . . . .17

## Matthew

5:23 . . . . . . . . .40
6 . . . . . . . . . . .62
6:5 . . . . . . .17, 40
6:6 . . . .14, 53, 54
6:7 . . . .19, 58, 59
6:10 . . . . . . . . .59
6:33 . . . . . .19, 29
7:7 . . . . . . . . . .28
7:7-11 . . . .47, 64
7:7-12 . . . . . . . .26
7:9-11 . . . . . . . .28
8:2,3 . . . . . . . . .14
8:13 . . . . . . . . .58
9:29 . . . . . . . . .58
13:5 . . . . . . . . .40
14:12 . . . . . . . .57
14:23 . . . . . . . .54
14:30 . . . . . . . .9
15:21-28 . . . . .17
15:22 . . . . . . . .57
15:25 . . . . . . . .9

18:19 ..53, 59, 64
21:12 .........33
21:22 .....11, 43,
              47, 58
23:14 .........40
26:41 .........14
26:42, 44 .....53
26:44 .........15
27:20 .........48

**Mark**

1:30 .........56
11:18 .........14
11:24 .....19, 29,
              58, 59
11:25 .........19
11:25,26 .....17
14:36 .........15

**Luke**

6:12 .........43
6:30 .........47
9:29 .........53
10:17 .........57
11:1 .........57
11:5-13 .......20
11:8 .........56
11:13 .........11
17:5 .........46
17:13, 17 ......52
18:1 ..33, 42, 59
18:5 .........56
18:7 .........42
18:11 .........52
18:13 .........52
21:36 .........59
22:41 .........15
22:42 .........15
22:43 .........15
22:44 .....15, 54
23:42 .........9
24:29 .........9
24:32 .........46

**John**

1:12,13 .......23

4:9,10 .......47
9:13 .........58
11:32 .........57
14:3 .........33
14:13 .....11, 59
14:13,14 ..19, 58,
              64
14:14 .....11, 33
15:16 .........11
15:3 .........33
15:7 ......11, 19,
              59, 64
15:7,8 .......14
16:23 .....11, 59
16:23,24 .....64
16:23,26 .....59
16:24 .....11, 59
16:26 .........11
17 .........62

**Acts**

1:14 .....42, 43
2:1,2 .........31
2:1-4 .........42
2:4 .........51
3:14 .........48
4:24-33 ......46
4:29 .........14
4:31 .....31, 51
6:25 .........14
8:15 .........53
9:11 ..31, 39, 51
9:11-20 .......46
10:1-6, 30 .....31
10:9 .........54
10:30 .........53
12:5 ..10, 17, 51
12:5-17 .......31
12:5-18 .......32
12:6 .........10
12:16 .........56
13:1-3 ...31, 53
13:3 .....51, 53
16:25 .........51
16:25-29 ......32
16:29 .........47

20:36 .........51
23:7 .........39
27 .........63
43:31 .........14

**Romans**

8:26 .....11, 16
10:8 .........53
12:12 ..26, 43, 59
15:30 .........54

**2 Corinthians**

1:11 .........51
5:7 .........53
5:20 .........23
7:1 .........56
12:7-9 .......17
12:8 .........63

**Galatians**

4:6 .........23

**Ephesians**

1 .............30
2:18 .........11
3 .............30
3:12 .........59
3:20 .....59, 64
6:18 ...14, 19, 59
6:18-19 ......55

**Philippians**

1:9-12 ......27
4:6 ......19, 33
4:6,7 ..14, 42, 46

**Colossians**

1:9 .........47
4:12 .....42, 43
4:2 ...19, 26, 43

**1 Thessalonians**

5:17 9, 14, 41, 42

**1 Timothy**

2:8 ......33, 56

**Hebrews**

2:17 .........52
4:16 .....12, 28,
              58, 59
5:7 ......15, 16
10:19, 22 .....58
10:19,20 .....59
10:22 .....58, 59
11:6 .........28
12:28 .........59

**James**

Book .........15
1:3-4 .........17
1:5 ......11, 47
1:5,6 .........16
1:6 ...11, 58, 59
1:8 .........61
4:3 ......17, 19,
              61, 63
5:13 .........15
5:14 .....15, 16
5:15 .....15, 53
5:16 ...15, 16, 64
5:17 ...14, 15, 58
5:17,18 ...14, 17
5:18 .....15, 58
5:19,20 .......16

**1 Peter**

1:7 .........17
3:7 .........17
5:6,7 .........17

**1 John**

3:22 .....11, 19,
              29, 58
5:14 .....29, 58
5:14,15 ...11, 19

**Jude**

20 .........16, 19

**Revelation**

1 .............54
2,3 .........50

# AN ALPHABET OF PERSONAL PRAYERS

*"Pray without ceasing" (1 Thess. 5:17).*

The Indians say that when a man kills a foe, the strength of the slain enemy enters into the victor's arm. We know that when the enemy of prayerlessness is killed, strength comes to the one who prays.

How many prayers we have recorded, and how many blessings there are which come to us as we pray. Let the following prayers illustrate.

"Abide with us."—The Prayer for Companionship (Luke 24:29).

"Bless me." —"Bless me, even me also, O my Father" (Gen. 27:34). Individual Prayer.

"Come unto me."—"Let Thy tender mercies come unto me, that I may live" (Ps. 119:77). Prayer for Life.

"Deliver me."—The Prayer for Victory (Ps. 31:15).

"Examine me."—A Prayer for Testing (Ps. 26:2).

Forgiveness.—A Prayer for Forgiveness (Ps. 25:18). "Forgive all my sins."

"Guide me."—The Prayer for Leading (Ps. 31:3). "For Thy Name's sake . . . guide me."

"Help me."—The Prayer for Aid (Matt. 15:25).

"Integrity . . . preserve me."—Prayer for uprightness (Ps. 25:21).

"Judge me."—Prayer for Discretion (Ps. 54:1).

"Keep me."—The Prayer for Preservation (Ps. 17:8).

"Lead me."—The Prayer for Direction (Ps. 139:24).

"Make me."—The Prayer for Adjustment (Ps. 119:35).

"Never be ashamed."—"Let me never be ashamed." A Prayer for Constancy (Ps. 71:1).

"Open mine eyes."—The Prayer for Illumination (Ps. 119:18).

"Preserve me."—The Prayer for Keeping (Ps. 16:1).

"Quicken me."—The Prayer for Revival (Ps. 119:25).

"Redeem me."—Prayer for Release (Ps. 26:11).

"Save me."—The Prayer for Rescue (Matt. 14:30).

"Teach me."—The Prayer for Instruction (Ps. 27:11).

"Unite my heart."—The Prayer for Communion (Ps. 86:11).

"Visit me."—A Prayer for Visitation (Ps. 106:4).

"Watch."—"Set a watch, O Lord, before my lips" (Ps. 141:3). Prayer for Prevention.

Xtremity.—"Remember me" (Luke 23:42).

The above prayers impress one in several ways. They are brief in utterance, direct in petition, personal in plea, humble in tone, dependent in faith, conscious of need, and earnest in manner.

F. E MARSH

# A PRAYER-MEETING IN APOSTOLIC TIMES

*Acts 12:5*

Peter had continued in prayer for the Church, and now the Church continues in prayer for him. There is blessed cooperation in the mystical body. It is a proof we are members of this body, if we bear one another's sorrows. Not pity, or condolence, or promise only, but really put our shoulder to the burden.

I.  **Observe, in This Case They Confined Their Efforts to Prayer**
Sometimes we find ourselves in such a position that we can do nothing but pray. Like Israel at the Red Sea: no power of theirs can make a passage through the waters, or defeat the oncoming legions; they can only wait on God. Or like Daniel in the lions' den, or Elijah when the rain was withheld. For such times we have a promise, "Ask, and ye shall receive."

II.  **Observe, They Continued in This Effort**
It was no formal or heartless prayer-meeting. They must have possessed strong faith. The case seemed hopeless. Tomorrow is fixed for Peter's death (v. 6). The hate of Herod is known to be malignant. James the apostle had been already slain.

III.  **They Reaped the Benefit**
The answer filled them with amazement.

The answer was superabundant.

Perhaps they had not prayed for his deliverance that night, or for his deliverance at all, but that he might glorify God in the fire.

The answer was speedy.

STEMS AND TWIGS

# ASKING

### I. Who to ask:
Our Heavenly Father. "Whatsoever ye shall *ask* of the *Father* in My name" (John 15:16).

### II. How to ask:
In the name of Christ. "Whatsoever ye shall *ask* in *My name, I will do it*" (John 14:13).

In the power of the Spirit. "Likewise the *Spirit* also *helpeth* our infirmities" (Rom. 8:26; Eph. 2:18).

In faith. "And all things, whatsoever ye shall *ask* in prayer, *believing*, ye shall receive" (Matt. 21:22; James 1:6).

### III. What to ask for:
Help of the Lord. "And Judah gathered themselves together, to *ask help of the Lord*" (2 Chron. 20:4).

Fullness of the Spirit. "How much more shall your heavenly Father give the *Holy Spirit* to them that *ask* Him" (Luke 11:13).

Fullness of joy. "*Ask*, and ye shall receive, that your *joy* may be *full*" (John 16:24).

Wisdom. "If any of you lack *wisdom*, let him *ask* of God" (James 1:5).

Anything. "If ye shall *ask anything* in My name, I will do it" (John 14:14).

### IV. The Condition:
Abiding in Christ. "If ye *abide* in Me, and My words abide in you, ye shall *ask* what ye will" (John 15:7; 1 John 3:22).

### V. Encouragements to ask:
Promise of Christ. "I say unto you, whatsoever ye shall *ask* the Father in My name, *He will give it*" (John 16:23).

He heareth us. "If we *ask* anything according to His will, *He heareth us*" (1 John 5:14,15).

Christ praying. "I *will pray* the Father for you" (John 16:26).

F. E. MARSH

# BOLDNESS AT THE THRONE

*"Let us therefore come boldly unto the throne of grace, that we may obtain mercy, and find grace to help in time of need" (Heb. 4:16).*

Prayer occupies a most important place in the life of the Christian. This verse is one of the sweetest of invitations to prayer.

### I.   Here Is Our Great Resort Described: "The throne of grace."

Once it was called "the mercy-*seat*," but now the "throne." In drawing near to God in prayer, we come:

A.   To God as a King, with reverence, confidence and submission.

B.   To One who gives as a King: therefore we ask largely and expectantly. He has riches of grace and power.

C.   To One who sits upon a throne "of grace," on purpose to dispense grace. It is His object in displaying Himself as King.

### II.   Here Is a Loving Exhortation: "Let us come."

A.   From Paul, a man like ourselves, but an experienced believer, who had much tried the power of prayer.

B.   From the whole church speaking in him.

C.   From the Holy Spirit; for the apostle spoke by inspiration. The Spirit, making intercession in us, says, "Let us come."

### III.   Here Is a Qualifying Adverb: "Let us come boldly."

Not proudly, presumptuously, nor with the tone of demand, for it is the throne; yet "boldly," for it is the throne *of grace*.

A.   We may come unreservedly, with all sorts of petitions.

B.   We may come freely, with simple words.

C.   We may come hopefully, knowing we will be heard.

D.   We may come fervently, with importunity of pleading.

### IV.   Here Is a Reason Given for Boldness: "Let us *therefore* come."

A.   We may come when we need great mercy, because of our sin. We may come when we have little grace.

B.   There are many other reasons for coming at once, and boldly. The character of God encourages us to be bold.

Our relation to Him as children gives us great freedom.

Christ is already given to us, and therefore God will deny us nothing.

C. The great reason of all for bold approach is in Jesus.
He once was slain, and the mercy-seat is sprinkled with
His blood.
He is risen and has justified us by His righteousness.
Let us come to the throne, when we are *sinful*, to find
*mercy*.
Let us come to the throne, when we are *weak*, to find
*help*.
Let us come to the throne, when we are *tempted*, to find
*grace*.

* When God enacts laws, He is on a throne of legislation: when He administers these laws, He is on a throne of government: when He tries His creatures by these laws, He is on a throne of judgment: but when He receives petitions, and dispenses favors, He is on a *throne of grace*.
A holy boldness, a chastened familiarity, is the true spirit of right prayer. It was said of Luther that, when he prayed, it was with as much reverence as if he prayed to an infinite God, and with as much familiarity as if he were speaking to his nearest friend. —G. S. Bowes.

* The word *boldly* signifies liberty without restraint. You may be free, for you are welcome. You may use freedom of speech. The word is so used in Acts 2:29 and 4:13. You have liberty to speak your minds freely, to speak all your heart, your concerns, and wants, and fears, and grievances. As others may not fetter you in speaking to God by prescribing what words you should use; so you need not restrain yourselves, but freely speak all that your condition requires. —David Clarkson.

* Obtaining mercy comes first; then finding grace to help in time of need. You cannot reverse God's order. You will not find grace to help in time of need till you have sought and found mercy to save. You have no right to reckon on God's help and protection and guidance, and all other splendid privileges which He promises to "the children of God by faith in Jesus Christ," until you have this first blessing, the mercy of God in Christ Jesus; for it is *"in"* Jesus Christ that all the promises of God are yea and Amen. —F. R. HAVERGAL.
CONDENSED FROM C. H. SPURGEON

# THE BELIEVER'S PRAYER

I. *What It Is*
   A. Empty Hand of need, as expressed in the parable of the friend at midnight (Matt. 8:2,3).
   B. Cry of Despair, bringing deliverance (Ps. 107:6, 13, 19, 28).
   C. Key to Open the storeroom of Heaven's supplies (Acts 43:31).
   D. Hedge of Protection keeping back the enemy (Neh. 6:9).
   E. Life's Blood coursing through the spiritual being, keeping all in health (Phil. 4:6,7).
   F. Prayer is the Companion of Praise (Acts 6:25).

II. *What It Does*
   A. Prayer Accomplishes things, as Elijah demonstrated (James 5:17).
   B. Prayer Concentrates the mind upon a given object, as Nehemiah illustrates (Neh. 4:9).
   C. Prayer Cleanses the heart and life, as David experienced (Ps. 51:10).
   D. Prayer Enables the witness to go forward with renewed courage (Acts 4:29).
   E. Prayer is the Soul of Revival, as the Psalmist recognized (Ps. 119:154).
   F. Prayer is One of the Weapons which is a part of the Christian's armor (Eph. 6:18).

III. *How to Pray*
   A. Pray *Secretly* in the closet of communion (Matt. 6:6).
   B. Pray *Watchfully* in the alertness of wakefulness (Matt. 26:41).
   C. Pray *Believingly* in the simplicity of faith (Mark 11:18).
   D. Pray *Unceasingly* in the continuance of well-doing (1 Thess. 5:17).
   E. Pray *Abidingly* in the will of God and in Christ (John 15:7,8).
   F. Pray *Directly* in the pointedness of definite petition (James 5:17,18).

CONDENSED FROM F. E. MARSH

## CHARACTERISTICS OF PRAYER IN JAMES 5

I. *Individual* prayer, "Let *him* pray" (v. 13).

II. *United* prayer, "Let *them* pray" (v. 14).

III. *Believing* prayer, "The prayer of *faith*" (v. 15).

IV. *Intercessory* prayer, "Pray *one for another*" (v. 16).

V. *Fervent* prayer, "the effectual *fervent* prayer" (v. 16).

VI. *Definite* prayer, "that it might not rain" (v. 17).

VII. *Effectual* prayer, "He prayed again, and the *heavens gave rain*" (v. 18).

J. L. S.

## CHRIST'S PRAYER IN GETHSEMANE

The characteristics of the prayer of Christ are:

I. It was a *lonely* prayer. He withdrew Himself about a stone's throw from His disciples, as He went to prayer (Luke 22:41).

II. It was a *humble* prayer. In Mark, we are told Christ "knelt," and in Matthew, that He fell upon His face. The attitude of His body is an indication of the posture of His spirit.

III. It was a *filial* prayer. He does not say here, as He did afterwards, "My God," etc., but "Abba Father." The former reminds of God's dealing in judgment with sin: the latter is the Father making known His will (Mark 14:36).

IV. It was an *earnest* prayer (Luke 22:44; Heb. 5:7).

V. It was a *repeated* prayer. He used "the same words" (Matt. 26:44).

VI. It was a *persevering* prayer. He prayed three times (Matt. 26:44).

VII. It was a *resigned* prayer. "Not My will," etc. (Luke 22:42). "'My will, not Thine, be done,' turned Paradise into a desert; and 'Thy will, not Mine be done,' turned the desert into a Paradise."

VIII. It was an *answered* prayer. In Luke 22:43, we are told an angel came and strengthened Him.

CONDENSED FROM F. E. MARSH

# EFFECTUAL FERVENT PRAYER

*"The effectual fervent prayer of a righteous man availeth much"*
*(James 5:16).*

James writes a great deal about prayer (James 1:5,6). It must be in faith, nothing wavering—a steady outstretched hand, looking, expecting, etc. He urges, draw nigh, etc. He is speaking in the context of prayer for others (v. 14), so in the text. Then he cites Elias, and refers, in the concluding verse, to prayer in its converting agency (vv. 19,20). Now prayer for others is the subject of the text.

I. The Man Who Prays.

"A righteous man." It does not mean an unfallen man, an innocent man, nor a perfect man—but a man,

A. In a *state of righteousness* or *justification*. Not in rebellion, not in enmity, but in a state of grace, accepted, justified.

B. A *renewed* man. One converted—born again.

C. An *obedient* man. One who serves God—who in heart and lip and life obeys God. Abel, Noah, Abraham, etc., were righteous, etc. So Zacchaeus, so the Baptist, etc. Now an unrighteous man does not pray or feel his need, etc. But,

D. He is a *loving* man. He loves others, and feels for, prays for, etc. Love is the very atmosphere of evangelical and experimental righteousness. Now see,

II. How He Prays.

In words, "effectual, fervent."

A. *Effectual* signifies inwrought. "Lord teach us!" Not mere outward—not saying or repeating, but put into the soul and inwrought, like veneering—like the works of a chronometer, like life in the body. Inwrought by "God's Holy Spirit" (Rom. 8:26; Jude 20).

B. *Fervent.* That is hot, earnest, vehement, etc., intense (see Heb. 5:7). It is said he prayed the "more earnestly." So of "Jacob," it is represented as "wrestling." These are the conditions or the features of the prayer spoken in the text. Observe,

III. The Obvious Certain Results.

"Availeth much," that is in general succeeds, obtains the answer, etc. Now notice,

A. The *limitation*. "Availeth much." Not all—not always—as a rule it succeeds—failure is the exception. Christ prayed for His murderers, but we don't think they were all saved. Aaron, we should think, prayed for his sons, but they perished. So Eli for his sons—so no doubt David, etc., so many. It is "much"—not always.

B. See how Scripture *helps* us to notable *instances* when *prayer* did manifestly *avail*. Jacob was anxious for his family, etc., expected to meet an angry brother (Gen. 32:24, etc.) Moses, the plague, the dying and dead, etc., the censer, etc. (Num. 16:6); so the overthrow of Amalek (so Ex. 32:10; 11:14). Now the case of Elias in the text (vv. 17,18). Daniel's prayer closed the mouth of the lions, brought an archangel from Heaven (Dan. 10:10). The people prayed for Peter, and the gate of the prison opened (Acts 12:5). Now in modern times prayer has been equally effectual. Instances numberless. Luther, Melancthon, Wesley, Muller of Bristol, etc.

Now let us see in conclusion,

1. The prerogative of prayer.
2. Its indispensable qualities; and,
3. Be assured of its general victory.

ADAPTED FROM JABEZ BURNS

---

## HINDRANCES TO PRAYER

*"That your prayers be not hindered"* (1 Peter 3:7).

Failure to obtain blessings sought in prayer not only robs and injures us and others, but dishonors God. We cannot, then, too carefully seek to know how our prayers may be hindered, or too earnestly strive to avoid such hindrances.

I. What reasons are given in the Word of God for withholding answers to some prayers?

See Isaiah 59:1,2; Mark 11:25,26; Psalm 138:6; Matthew 6:5; James 4:3; 1 Samuel 16:7; Psalm 66:18.

II. Is the fact that the results of prayer which are not immediately seen any proof that it is not, or will not be answered?

See and compare Job 30:20 with 42:8; Matthew 15:21-28; 2 Corinthians 12:7-9; 1 Peter 1:7; James 1:3-4.

III. What is the right course when the answer to prayer is or seems to be delayed?

See 1 Peter 5:6,7; Daniel 9:23; Isaiah 58:3-14; Genesis 32:26, with Hosea 12:4-6; Psalm 40:1, and 27:14. SELECTED

# THE HYPOCRITE'S PRAYER

*"Will he always call upon God?" (Job 27:10).*

A hypocrite may be a very neat imitation of a Christian. He professes to know God, to converse with Him, to be dedicated to His service, and to invoke His protection; he even practices prayer or at least feigns it. Yet the cleverest counterfeit fails somewhere, and may be discovered by certain signs. The test is here, "Will he always call upon God?"

I. **Will He Pray at All Seasons of Prayer?**

Will he pray in private? Or is he dependent upon the human eye and the applause of men?

Will he pray if forbidden? Daniel did so. Will he?

Will he pray in business? Will he practice spontaneous prayer? Will he look for hourly guidance?

Will he pray in pleasure? Will he have a holy fear of offending with his tongue? Or will company make him forget his God?

Will he pray in darkness of soul? Or will he sulk in silence?

II. **Will He Pray Importunately?**

If no answer comes, will he persevere? Is he like the brave horse who will pull at a post at his master's bidding?

If a rough answer comes, will he plead on? Does he know how to wrestle with the angel, and give tug for tug?

If no one else prays, will he plead against wind and tide?

If God answers him by disappointment and defeat, will he feel that delays are not denials, and still pray?

III. **Will He Continue to Pray Throughout the Whole of Life?**

The hypocrite soon gives up prayer under certain circumstances. If he is in trouble, he will not pray, but will run to human helpers. If he gets out of trouble, he will not pray, but quite forget his vows.

If men laugh at him, he will not dare to pray.

If men smile on him, he will not care to pray.

A. He grows weary. He can make a spurt, but he cannot keep it up. Short prayers are sweet to him.

B. He grows secure. Things go well and he sees no need of prayer; or he is too holy to pray.

• We have heard of a child who said her prayers, and then

added, "Good-bye, God; we are all going to Saratoga, and pa and ma won't go to meeting, or pray any more till we come back again." We read that many who go on holiday, give God the go-by in much the same manner.                    —Guthrie

•   Ahaz will not ask a sign, even when God bids him, lest he should tempt the Lord (Isa. 7:10, 12); a great piece of modesty in show, but a sure symptom of infidelity. He would not ask a sign because he could not believe the thing; not to avoid troubling of God, but himself. He seems very mannerly, but shows himself very impertinent.

Thus, this hypocrite will serve God only by fits and starts, when he himself feels so disposed. He never troubles God unless God troubles him. In health, wealth, peace, he can comfort himself. He never prays but in trouble; in his affliction he will seek God early (Hosea 5:15). God is fain to go away, and return to His place, else this man would never look after Him. When God has touched him, he acquaints God with his misery, but when times grow better with him, he excludes God from his mirth.                    —Samuel Crook.

CONDENSED FROM C. H. SPURGEON

---

# IN ORDER THAT OUR PRAYERS MAY BE ANSWERED

   I.   We Must ask in the name of Jesus (John 14:13,14).

   II.   We Must be abiding in Him and His Word in us (John 15:7).

   III.   We Must be keeping His commandments (1 John 3:22).

   IV.   We Must give thanks at the same time (Phil. 4:6).

   V.   We Must be watching for answers (Col. 4:2).

   VI.   We Must speak spiritual things *first* (Matt. 6:33).

   VII.   We Must pray for all saints at the same time (Eph. 6:18).

   VIII.   We Must seek God's mind (Jude 20, Eph. 6:18).

   IX.   We Must have no hard feelings toward *anyone* (Mark 11:25).

   X.   We Must Not "Babble" (Matt. 6:7).

   XI.   We Must Not ask for fleshly desire (James 4:3).

   XII.   We Must Not doubt; God will keep His word (Mark 11:24; 1 John 5:14,15).                    SELECTED

# IMPORTUNITY IN PRAYER IN THE LIFE OF JESUS

*Luke 11:5-13*

Jesus Christ was emphatically a man of prayer. Rising a great while before day, He went into a solitary place and prayed. In the evening after His arduous labors, He retired to a mountain and spent the whole night in prayer. Before setting apart the twelve apostles, He spent some time in special supplications. When on the mount of transfiguration, it was as He prayed, that the fashion of His countenance was altered, and His raiment became white and glistening. He prayed at the grave of Lazarus. He prayed for Peter by name; and on the memorable night in which He was betrayed, He prayed for all the disciples, and not for them only, but also for all who should believe on Him through their word. In the garden, when He underwent the baptism of blood, He offered up prayers and supplications, with strong crying and tears; again and again He prayed, going and returning, and saying the same words. And having lived a life of prayer, He died a death at prayer, crying on behalf of His blood-thirsty foes, "Father forgive them, for they know not what they do."

In exhorting His disciples to pray, the Savior, therefore, only exhorted them to follow His example. Whatever He preached He practiced; and all the commands He gave were strikingly enforced by His own habitual conduct.

Among the many representations which are given of this important duty, that contained in the words before us is one of the most instructive and encouraging. Three things are set forth in them, which are well-deserving of our consideration. We have,

## I. A Case Supposed

"And He said unto them, Which of you shall have a friend, and shall go unto him at midnight," etc. The circumstance referred to was probably of frequent occurrence, as journeys in the East are often performed in the night, on account of the oppressive heat of the day. This person had no provisions to set before his friend, who had arrived unexpectedly; he, therefore, applied to a neighbor to borrow three loaves, or cakes. At first no disposition was shown to act the part of a friend in need; but the applicant was resolved not to leave the place until his request was granted; and at length, in consequence of his urgency, he succeeded. In the parable of the unjust judge a similar case is described. He granted the request of the poor widow, not from a principle of justice, or a feeling of compassion, but because her continual coming wearied him.

It is evident that the Savior did not justify the motive in either of these instances. He simply referred to them for the purpose of showing how earnestness and perseverance secure success, even under the most unfavorable circumstances. And if reluctant and hardhearted men thus yield to the influence of importunity, how much more will the blessed God, who delights in bestowing benefits upon the needy, grant the requests of those who call upon Him!

II.   An Exhortation Addressed

"And I say unto you, Ask, and it shall be given you; seek, and ye shall find," etc. We have here,

A.  *The true nature of prayer.* It is simply a matter of asking and receiving. There are some who view prayer altogether in reference to its influence upon the minds of those who engage in it. That it has such an influence is undoubted; but over and above its soothing, elevating, purifying effect, there are direct and positive blessings to be looked for in answer to our requests. The labor of the farmer is beneficial to him; in itself it is so; being conducive to his health and strength—to the invigoration of his powers both of body and mind. But it is not on that account that he labors. He expects an actual crop; and he goes forth and sees, first the blade, then the ear, and then the full corn in the ear. And so with prayer. Its action and exercise are beneficial; but if there be any truth in the representations of Scripture, there are real, actual, palpable, unmistakable answers to prayer as well. There is something to be distinctly sought on the one hand, and something to be as distinctly obtained on the other.

B.  *The proper spirit of prayer.* It is here plainly implied that we are to ask with earnestness and importunity. What good are those petitions which are cold and heartless? It is "the effectual, fervent prayer of the righteous that availeth much." And it is not enough to be earnest for the moment. Our fervor must not resemble a blaze of straw, which soon goes out. We must beware of restraining prayer before God. We must pray, and not faint.

C.  *The certain success of prayer.* "It *shall* be given you"— "ye *shall* find"—"it *shall* be opened." And the experience of God's people in every age confirms the truth of these decisive expressions.

"This is the confidence that we have in Him, that, if we ask anything according to His will, He heareth us: and if we know that He hear us, whatsoever we ask, we know that we have the petitions that we desired of Him" (1 John 5:15). And who was it that bore this testimony? It was one who lived a long life of changes and difficulties. It was based upon the experience of the apostle John, who outlived the rest of his brethren.

### III.   A Touching Argument Employed

"If a son shall ask bread of any of you that is a father, will he give him a stone? or if he ask for a fish, will he for a fish give him a serpent? or if he shall ask an egg, will he offer him a scorpion? If ye then being evil," etc. How touching and conclusive this is. It is addressed to "any of you that is a father." As if it had been said, Can any of you refuse what your children from necessity ask of you, or give them what would be useless or injurious? On the contrary, will not your hearts be drawn out to them in the warmest and tenderest concern, and will not you be disposed to fulfill to the utmost of your ability, all their wants and wishes? Now, mark the irresistible inference which the Savior draws. "If ye then being evil," possessors of a nature which is at best imperfect, and having consequently much corruption clinging to your highest feelings, and worthiest doings: "If ye then being evil, know how to give good gifts unto your children; how much more shall your heavenly Father"—in whom no defect exists, and in whom no imperfection can be found—"how much more shall your heavenly Father give the Holy Spirit to them that ask Him?" It is inquired, How much more? As much more as God is higher than man; as much more as God is holier than man; as much as God is better than man—so much more will He give the Holy Spirit to them that ask Him.

Let us resolve, then, to test the truth of this gracious assurance. If we do so, we shall find that it is a faithful promise, and that it has never failed yet.

SELECTED

# JACOB'S PRAYER

*Genesis 22*

There are six things we note about Jacob's prayer.

I.   Jacob's fear of his brother's anger prompted it (v. 11).

Jacob was fearful because of his mean conduct toward his brother and cringes before Esau like a guilty culprit supplicating for mercy. Note that any punishment we unrighteously inflict upon others is sure to come back upon our own heads. But for all that, the Lord listened to Jacob's cry. What a God of grace with whom we have to do!

II.   Jacob's relationship to God is his plea in prayer (v. 9).

He pleads his relationship to God in the words, "O God of my father, . . .". If we know God as our Father, the right way in speaking to Him is to call Him "Father" (John 1:12,13; Gal. 4:6). But if we have not answered God's prayer (2 Cor. 5:20), how can we expect Him to answer ours?

III.   God's promise is Jacob's argument in prayer (vv. 9, 12).

Jacob pleads two "I wills" of God. When our prayers depend on God's promise, He will perform His word. Spurgeon says, "Prayer should be pillared on promises, and pinnacled with praises."

IV.   Jacob's prayer is mingled with confession (v. 10).
All God's servants have ever confessed their unworthiness.

V.   Jacob's prayer is perfumed with praise (v. 10).

Jacob acknowledges the mercy he had received from God, and gives praise. A thank*ful* man is full of blessing, while a thank*less* man is full of complaint. If we bless God with our praises, He will bless us with His mercies.

VI.   Jacob's prayer is definite, personal, and answered (v. 11).

"Deliver me," Jacob cries, and the sequel shows how graciously God granted his prayer. His prayer was short and to the point, and it brought a speedy answer.

VII.   Because He promises to do it. "He shall be holy unto thee, for I, the Lord, which sanctify you, am holy" (Lev. 21:8).

We may be sure of this, that when God tells us to be, to do, and to suffer, He will meet our need, even as in the case of Paul, who prayed thrice that the thorn might be removed, but the Lord answered by saying, "My grace is sufficient for thee."                F. E. MARSH

# NEHEMIAH'S PRAYER

*Nehemiah 1:1-11*

In the character of Nehemiah there is much to be admired. He was evidently a man of high integrity, as appears from the position which he held, that of the king's cup-bearer. Only a thoroughly trustworthy person would be permitted to occupy such a post, inasmuch as the lives of eastern monarchs were in constant danger from the aspiring courtiers by whom they were surrounded; and as one of the most common methods of causing death, in ancient times, was by mixing some poisonous ingredient with the wine that was drank, it is quite obvious that no one would be entrusted with this office in the king's household, who was likely to be influenced by the bribes of the king's enemies.

But, in addition to his strict integrity, he was a man of sincere and fervent piety. Of this he gave various proofs, especially by answering to the psalmist's description—"for this shall every one that is godly *pray* unto thee." Very frequently did he give himself unto prayer, and it is thus we find him engaged in the present chapter.

## I. The Occasion of This Prayer

It is stated in the first three verses. "The words of Nehemiah, the son of Hachaliah. And it came to pass," etc. It is said of the Redeemer—"In all their affliction He was afflicted"; and His people are like-minded with Him in this respect. They feel for others; and hence the miserable condition of his brethren awoke the tenderest sympathy in the breast of this man of God. He also loved Zion, and the information he received concerning the wall of Jerusalem being broken down, and the gates thereof being burnt with fire, filled his soul with sadness.

## II. The Being to Whom His Prayer Is Addressed

"And it came to pass when I heard these words that I sat down and wept, and mourned certain days, and fasted, and prayed before the God of heaven, and said, I beseech thee, O Lord God of heaven, the great and terrible God, that keepeth covenant and mercy for them that love Him and observe His commandments." Those among whom he dwelt were accustomed in their distress to invoke the aid of their heathen deities; but, knowing full well how vain it was to seek relief from such lying vanities, he called upon the God of heaven. In applying to Him he felt assured that he was not praying to a god who could not save.

There were two aspects of His glorious character in which he more especially regarded Him.

A. As great and terrible.

B. As faithful and gracious.

The former view filled his mind with sacred awe, the latter inspired him with hope and confidence.

## III. The Penitential Spirit Which It Breathes

"Let Thine ear now be attentive, and Thine eyes open, I pray before Thee now, day and night, for the children of Israel, which we have sinned against Thee; both I and my father's house have sinned. We have dealt very corruptly against Thee," etc. When we appear before God, it should be with confession and deep humiliation. Thus David prayed, and Jeremiah, and especially Daniel (9:4-11).

## IV. The Powerful Plea Which Is Employed

"Remember, I beseech Thee, the word that Thou commandest Thy servant Moses, saying, If ye transgress, I will scatter you abroad among the nations; but if ye return unto Me," etc. If we ask anything according to His will, we may feel assured that He will hear us; and that must be according to His will which He has promised to do. "Remember," says the psalmist, "Thy word unto Thy servant, upon which Thou hast caused me to hope." And this was the argument of Nehemiah; he pleads that God would accomplish what He had formerly declared.

## V. The Earnest Importunity with Which It Is Presented

"O Lord, I beseech Thee, let now Thine ear be attentive," etc. He had asked before for the same thing; but, instead of it being a vain repetition, it indicates how intense were his earnestness and anxiety. It is the fervent prayer of the righteous man, that availeth much; that which is cold and heartless, availeth nothing. "If the arrow of prayer," says an old writer, "is to enter heaven, we must draw it from a soul full bent."

SELECTED

# PERSISTENT PRAYER

*"Continue in prayer" (Col. 4:2; see Rom. 12:12).*

It has truly been said that prayer is the evidence of spiritual life; the necessary result of regeneration; the fruit of the indwelling Spirit; a glorious privilege of the sons and daughters of God; and a solemn duty obligatory on all the saints of the Most High. But there are many things opposed to its steady, fervent exercise, and many ways by which prayer may be hindered, or become formal, or be interrupted, or cease; so the necessity of feeling the force of the text, to "Continue in prayer." See:

I. **What This Continuance in Prayer Involves.**

A. *That* the *exercise* of *prayer* has *begun*. It is not to commence prayer, that is assumed as a fact, a reality, but still to cultivate it and to attend to it. Then it signifies:

B. To *continue in* the *habit* of *prayer*. Cherish it as an essential condition of spiritual life, as breathing is to the natural life, or the heartbeat is to continuance of existence, or as eating is, etc.

C. Continuance in the *spirit* of prayer. There may be the form, the words, etc., and yet no spirit. All may be cold and merely nominal; the corpse without the soul.

D. To *continue* in *all* the essential parts of prayer—in adoration, confession, pleading, supplication, intercession with thanksgiving.

E. To continue in the *various kinds* of prayer—secret, or closet devotion, family, or household prayer, etc. Notice:

II. **How We May Obey the Injunction.**

A. By *cherishing* a *sense* of our *constant need*. No prayer without this; this will ever lead to prayer.

B. By *seeking* the Holy *Spirit's quickening aid* in *prayer*. Thus we shall be stirred up, and inflamed, saved from drowsiness and apathy.

C. By *remembering* the *great* and *precious* promises in *relation* to *prayer*. They abound everywhere in the sacred volume, especially in the Psalms, Gospels, Epistles, and Matthew 7:7-12.

D. By *setting before* us the *illustrious examples* of persistent prayer; as Jacob, Moses, Elijah, David, Daniel, etc., the Disciples, especially Jesus.

E. By a *recollection* of the *good* things *we* have *realized* by *prayer.* Our own experience at the commencement of the Christian life, in various seasons of need, trouble, perplexity. Observe:

### III. Why We Should Continue in Prayer.

A. It is a *Divine obligation.* We are called to it, exhorted, commanded. Not to do so would be disobedient, rebellion, etc.

B. *It is linked with our very safety.* We can only stand, or advance, or labor, or avoid the perils around us, or overcome our foes by prayer.

C. It is *indispensable* to *our happiness.* The renewed soul must pray; it would be gloom, sadness, misery without it. It brings us to God's gracious presence, smiling face; it banishes clouds, surrounds the soul with joy and sunshine and heaven.

D. It is an *essential* of *salvation.* "Whosoever shall call," etc. We cannot conceive of a soul being saved without it. Prayerlessness would be a sign of self-reprobation and destruction.

### Application

1. A word to the prayerless.
2. Exhortation to God's people as to unceasing prayer. Praying always with all prayer, etc.
3. As to the sweetness of the exercise, and greatness of the privilege.
4. As to its being a test of our true spiritual condition.

JABEZ BURNS

---

## PAUL'S PRAYER FOR THE PHILIPPIANS

*"And this I pray, that your love,"* etc. (Phil. 1:9-12).

The value of intercessory prayer.

Three petitions included in this prayer. That they might exhibit:

### I. An Intelligent, Discerning Love.

"That your love may abound yet more and more in knowledge and in all judgment; that ye may approve things that are excellent."

### II. A Pure, Inoffensive Spirit.

"That ye may be sincere and without offense. . . ."

### III. A Useful, Beneficent Life.

"Being filled with the fruits of righteousness, which are by Jesus Christ unto the glory and praise of God." SELECTED

---

# PETITION

Supplication, or petition, means *prayer for oneself* as distinguished from *intercession*, which is *prayer for others*. This naturally follows worship and confession, for, if the revelation of God to our hearts in worship leads us to confession of sin and need, in petition we will at once make appeal for the supply of that personal need, and claim for ourselves the divine provision. Bearing in mind, then, that we are now considering prayer in relation to our own personal need, let us think first of all of:

## I. *The Pledge for Offering Our Petitions*

Of the many passages which encourage us to come to our loving Father and tell Him all that is in our heart, one or two must suffice here: "Come boldly unto the throne of grace, that we may obtain mercy and find grace to help in time of need" (Heb. 4:16). Every word in this verse is significant. "Come," that is one of the greatest, as it is one of the simplest words in the Bible. "Boldly," that is, with courage, candor, and confidence. "To the throne of grace," which is none other than the throne of God, for there is nothing higher. "That we may obtain mercy," a clear reference to our need in view of the *past*, and suggestive of the atoning merits (mercy) and the claim of faith (obtain). "And find grace to help in time of need." This has reference to *future* need, and is suggestive of the storing of grace against need.

## II. *The Conditions of Prevailing Prayer*

God may not be approached anyhow and by anybody. The divine promises to those who would pray, rest upon the fulfillment of certain conditions:

A. We must have confidence in prayer as a practical power (Heb. 11:6), otherwise we are simply beating the air, or pouring water through a sieve when we pray. If we do not believe that prayer changes things, then, in the interests of honesty, let us abandon it. Dr. Schauffler has well said: "Prayer is either a prodigious *force* or a disgraceful *farce*. If a *farce*, you may pray much, and get little; if a *force*, you may pray little and get much." Faith is absolutely essential to effectuality.

B. We must be frank and earnest in the presence of God (Matt. 7:7). Is there something you need? Ask for it. The Apostle James says, "Ye have not because ye ask not."

C. We must be always definite in our requests (Matt. 7:9-

11). Indefinite petitions can hardly expect more than indefinite answers: if we are vague with God, He will be vague with us.

D.   We must offer our petitions in faith (Mark 11:24). This is a remarkable passage, the point of which is too often overlooked. Whatsoever things we desire when we pray, we are to believe that we do, at the time, receive them, and in God's good time we shall receive them; in other words, we are to receive the thing in order to get it.

E.   We must ask according to the will of God (1 John 5:14). But the problem with thousands of the Lord's people is to know what is the will of God; and we are constantly asked, "How can one know?" Perhaps another verse in this Epistle will help to resolve that difficulty (1 John 3:22): "Whatsoever we ask, we receive of Him, because we keep His commandments, and do those things that are pleasing in His sight." If we do the will of God, we shall know it, for every step taken in obedience to His Word lets loose fresh light. There are very many more conditions of prevailing prayer which should be sought out and responded to, but these may serve just to show the way.

But we should search out also:

### III.   *The Promises Made to Him Who Prays*

How many and magnificent are the promises which God has made to those who humbly and trustfully draw near to Him. It has been pointed out that all the unconditioned phrases are applied to prayer: "Whosoever," "whatsoever," "wheresoever," "whensoever," "all," "any," "every"; that no one should be left in doubt as to the largeness of the Divine heart, or the readiness of the Divine will.

### IV.   *The Proper Subjects for Daily Prayer*

One passage of Scripture will suffice to guide us in this matter. "Seek ye first the kingdom of God, and His righteousness, and all these things shall be added unto you" (Matt. 6:33). Two classes of things are referred to—things spiritual, and things temporal. Not the spiritual only, and not the temporal first. Our gracious Father has made provision for the whole of our need, but there is a priority of some things over others. Our spiritual need is our supreme need, because our souls are of more consequence than our bodies; and yet, in our prayers, we give more attention to the latter than to the former.

Have you ever studied the prayers of the Apostle Paul? Perhaps the most interesting feature of them is their intense spirituality. What he is concerned about is that he may have the spirit of wisdom and revelation in the knowledge of Christ; that the eyes of his heart might be enlightened; that he might know what was the issue of his holy calling, and what the riches of the glory of Christ's inheritance in him and all the saints, and how exceeding great is His power toward and in those who believe (Eph. 1). He longs also to be strengthened with might, by the Holy Spirit, in the inner man: to be rooted and grounded in love, and to apprehend what is the breadth, and length, and depth, and height of the Divine love, which he is conscious must transcend all human knowledge (Eph. 3).

Tell God, therefore, all you need, spiritual and temporal, and rest assured that He Who is so careful with our souls will not be careless about our bodies.

One other thing claims our attention, namely:

### V. *The Practical Outcome of Our Requests*

Does God answer prayer? Surely that is a proper subject of inquiry, and one to which every Christian should be able to give an unhesitating answer. Of course God answers prayer; and if the testimonies of all His people throughout the ages were to be written, in the language of St. John, "I suppose that even the world itself could not contain the books that should be written." Abram and Moses, David, Elijah and Daniel, and Paul got their prayers answered, and so may you and I. The God of George Muller is our God also, and will honor our obedience and faith, as He honored his.

But we may hold much too narrow an idea as to what constitutes an answer to prayer. This subject receives ample illustration in the fifth chapter of Mark's Gospel, where three prayers are answered, but all differently. First, there is the prayer of the demons, to be allowed to go into the swine. Then, the prayer of the healed man, to be allowed to accompany Jesus. And finally, the prayer of Jairus, that Jesus would come and heal his daughter.

History is not without illustration also, of desire being unheeded in the granting of petitions. We read of Israel that, "He gave them their request, but sent leanness into their soul." God in His mercy neglects the terms of many of our prayers, because He sees how injurious to us would be the fulfillment. And then, again, the truer our prayers are, the nearer will the correspondence be between the desire of the heart and the request of the lips, so that Christ may answer both.

CONDENSED FROM W. GRAHAM SCROGGIE

# POWER IN PRAYER

*"When they had prayed the place was shaken" (Acts 4:31).*

"If," said a plain, blunt farmer, in referring to a minister's prayer, "any son of mine should ask a favor as tamely as that minister spoke to his 'Father in heaven,' I should give him the stick."

Oh, that we might realize to the full:

> "Prayer is the mightiest force that men can wield;
> A power to which omnipotence doth yield;
> A privilege unparalleled—a way
> Whereby the Almighty Father can display
> His interest in His children's need and care."

We see what a potent force was in the life of the early Christians. They lifted themselves up to the Lord in earnest prayers, and He moved them on by His Living power. What a power prayer is:

I.   Prayer is a *Procuring Power*. It was in answer to and while they, the saints, were praying, the power of Pentecost came (Acts 2:1,2).

II.  Prayer is a *Qualifying Power*. After the early Christians had prayed, they "spake the Word of God with boldness" (Acts 4:31).

III. Prayer is an *Evidencing Power*. The mark by which Ananias was to recognize Saul of Tarsus as a believer was, "Behold he prayeth" (Acts 9:11).

IV.  Prayer is an *Enlightening Power*. Of Cornelius it is said he "prayed to God alway," and the result was he had a vision (Acts 10:1-6, 30).

V.   Prayer is a *Liberating Power*. When Peter was shut up in prison, it was the prayers of the saints that brought him out of it (Acts 12:5-17).

VI.  Prayer is the *Consecrating Power*. While the early church at Antioch prayed and fasted, the Holy Spirit consecrated Paul and Barnabas to the sacred service of the Gospel (Acts 13:1-3).

VII. Prayer is an *Awakening Power*. The prayers of Paul and Silas were the cause of the earthquake, which caused a heart-quake in the heart of the Philippian jailer (Acts 16:25-34).

F. E. MARSH

# PRAYER

*"The God that answereth" (1 Kings 18:24).*

We shall have no doubt that God answers prayer, if we accept what God says in His Word. Bishop Barnes says:

"I myself have no doubts as to the value of prayer." He is further reported, in his Gifford Lectures, in the *Aberdeen Press*, to have said: "A merely mechanical theory of the Universe I reject. God rules the world: the laws of Nature are His laws, and in no way constrain His freedom. Thus there is no reason to believe that God cannot grant favorable answers to the crudest petitionary prayers; our experience alone can determine whether He thus acts as we seek His aid.

"I should even hesitate to declare that petitions for rain or fair weather were necessarily unavailing, there is no theoretical reason why God should not hearken to such prayer. I would pray for a friend's recovery from sickness with the knowledge that such prayers are often of no avail, and yet with hope that God in His goodness would grant my petition. With great confidence would I pray for strength against temptation, whether I myself or some other were in need."

God not only answers by fire, as He did on Mount Carmel, but He answers in a variety of other ways, as the following seven instances, recorded in the Bible, illustrate.

I. By *Healing* from sickness, as in the case of Hezekiah (2 Kings 20:1-7).

II. By *Deliverance* from danger, as demonstrated in Hezekiah's victory over Sennacherib (2 Chron. 32:20-22).

III. By *Success* in carrying through an enterprise, as He did Nehemiah, in building the wall of Jerusalem (Neh. 4:4-6).

IV. By *Power*, as at Pentecost, when the power of the Spirit came on the disciples (Acts 2:1-4).

V. By an *Earthquake*, as evidenced when the prison at Philippi was shaken, Paul and Silas were freed (Acts 16:25-29).

VI. By an *Angel*, as seen in Peter's case, when he was brought out of prison (Acts 12:5-18).

VII. By *Rain*, as revealed in the downpour which deluged the land through Elijah's petitions (James 5:17,18).

F. E. MARSH

## PRAYER: AN ATTITUDE

*"I will therefore that men pray everywhere, lifting up holy hands,
without wrath and doubting" (1 Tim. 2:8).*

Benjamin Jowett says of prayer: "Prayer is an act, performed at set times, in certain forms of words; but prayer is also a spirit which need not be expressed in words—the spirit of contentment and resignation, of active goodness and benevolence, of modesty and truthfulness." In other words, prayer is an attitude of heart, as well as an act of worship, in expressed need. This heart attitude is expressed in many ways in the Psalms.

I. It is a waiting upon the Lord in *Dependence* (Ps. 27:14).

II. It is a being still before the Lord in *Contentment* (Ps. 62:1, margin).

III. It is an expectation from the Lord in *Reliance* (Ps. 62:5).

IV. It is a delight in the Lord in *Communion* (Ps. 37:4).

V. It is a resting on the Lord in *Patience* (Ps. 37:7).

VI. It is a trusting with the Lord in *Service* (Ps. 37:3).

VII. It is a rising to the Lord in *Satisfaction* (Ps. 91).

F. E. MARSH

## PRAYER AND PROMISE

|  | *Prayer* | *Promise* |
|---|---|---|
| Cleanse Me | (Ps. 51:2) | (John 15:3) |
| Keep Me | (Ps. 67:8) | (1 Sam. 2:9) |
| Guide Me | (Ps. 31:3) | (Ps. 32:8) |
| Receive Me | (Ps. 49:15) | (John 14:3) |

RITCHIE

## PRAYER

The place for Prayer, "Everywhere" (1 Tim. 2:8)
The time for Prayer, "Always" (Luke 18:1)
Subjects for Prayer, "Everything" (Phil. 4:6)
Answers to Prayer, "All Things" (Matt. 21:12)
Conditions of Prayer, "In My Name" (John 14:14)           RITCHIE

# PRAYER ENCOURAGED

*"Call unto Me, and I will answer thee, and shew thee great and mighty things which thou knowest not" (Jer. 33:3).*

This is a prison verse: let those who are spiritually in prison prize it.

This was the second time the Lord had spoken to the prophet while in the dungeon. God does not forsake His people because they oppose the world, nor even when they are put into prison. Rather, He doubles His visits when they are in double trouble. The text belongs to every afflicted servant of God. It encourages him in a threefold manner:

I.   To Continue in Prayer. "Call unto Me!"

    A.   Pray, though you have prayed (see Jer. 32:16ff).

    B.   Pray though you are still in prison after prayer. If deliverance tarries, make your prayers the more importunate.

    C.   Pray; for the Word of the Lord commands this.

    D.   Pray; for the Holy Spirit prompts you, and helps you.

II.   To Expect Answers to Prayer. "I will answer thee. . . ."
The Lord will answer us because:

    A.   He has appointed prayer, and made arrangements for its presentation and acceptance. He could not have meant it to be a mere farce: that were to treat us as fools.

    B.   He prompts, encourages, and quickens prayer; and surely He would never mock us by exciting desires which He never meant to gratify. Such a thought well-nigh blasphemes the Holy Spirit, Who ignites and even inscribes prayer in the heart.

    C.   He has given His promise in the text; and it is often repeated elsewhere: He cannot lie or deny Himself.

III.   To Expect Great Things as Answers to Prayer. "I will shew thee great and mighty things."

Read Jeremiah 32 from verse 18, and learn from it that we are to look for things.

    A.   Great in counsel: full of wisdom and significance.

    B.   Divine things: "I will shew thee." These are enumerated in the verses which follow the text, even to the end of the chapter: such as these:

        Health and cure (v. 6).
        Liberation from captivity (v. 7).

Forgiveness of iniquity (v. 8).
See how sufferers may win unexpected deliverances.
See how workers may achieve surprising marvels.
See how seekers may find more than they dare expect.

- A young engineer was being examined, and this question was put to him: "Suppose you have a steam-pump constructed for a ship, under your own supervision, and know that everything is in perfect order, yet, when you throw out the hose, it will not draw; what should you think?" "I should think, sir, there must be a defect somewhere." "But such a conclusion is not admissible; for the supposition is that everything is perfect, and yet the pump will not work." "Then, sir," replied the student, "I should look over the side of the ship to see if the river had run dry." Even so, it would appear that if true prayer is not answered, the nature of God must have changed.
God's praying people get to know much more of His mind than others; like as John, by weeping, got the book opened; and Daniel, by prayer, had the king's secret revealed unto him in a night vision. —Trapp.

- Sir Walter Raleigh was one day asking a favor from Queen Elizabeth. The latter said to him, "Raleigh, when will you leave off begging?" To which he answered, "When your Majesty leaves off giving." Ask great things of God. Expect great things from God. Let His past goodness make us "instant in prayer."
—*New Cyclopaedia of Illustrative Anecdote*.

- The dungeon of the Mamertine, where a probable tradition declares that Paul was for a while confined, is entered through a round hole in the floor of another dungeon above. The uppermost apartment is dark enough, but the lower one is darkness itself, so that the apostle's imprisonment was of the severest kind.

  We noticed, however, a strange fact: in the hard floor there is a beautiful fountain of clear crystal water, which doubtless was as fresh in Paul's day as it is now; of course the faithful believe the fountain to be miraculous; we who are not so credulous of traditions rather see in it a symbol full of instruction: there never was a dungeon for God's servants which was without its well of consolation.

CONDENSED FROM C. H. SPURGEON

# PRAYER FOR THE CHURCH

*"Now, therefore, O our God, hear the prayer of Thy servant,
and his supplications, and cause Thy face to shine upon
Thy sanctuary that is desolate, for the Lord's sake" (Dan. 9:17).*

This true-hearted man lived not for himself. Daniel was a fervent lover of his country.

His prayer is instructive to us. It suggests our fervent entreaties for the church of God in these days.

I. **The Holy Place.** "Thy sanctuary."

The temple was typical, and for our edification we shall read the text as if the spiritual house had been meant. There are many points in the type worthy of notice, but these may suffice:

A. The temple was unique; and as there could only be one temple for Jehovah, so there is but one church.

B. The temple was the result of great cost and vast labor; so was the church built by the Lord Jesus at a cost which can never be estimated.

C. The temple was the shrine of God's indwelling.

D. The temple was the place of His worship.

E. The temple was the throne of His power: His Word went forth from Jerusalem; there He ruled His people, and routed His foes.

II. **The Earnest Prayer.** "Cause Thy face to shine upon Thy sanctuary that is desolate."

A. It rose above all selfishness. This was his one prayer, the center of all his prayers.

B. It cast itself upon God. "O our God."

C. It was a confession that he could do nothing of himself. Honest men do not ask God to do what they can do themselves.

D. It asked a comprehensive boon. "Cause Thy face to shine." This would mean many things which we also implore for the church of God.

    1. Ministers in their places, faithful in their service.

    2. Truth proclaimed in its clarity. God's face cannot shine upon falsehood or equivocation.

    3. Delight in fellowship.

    4. Power in testimony. When God is pleased His Word is mighty.

III.  The Consistent Conduct. This is suggested by such a prayer.

A.  Let us lay it earnestly to heart. Whether for joy or sorrow, let the condition of the church concern us deeply.

B.  Let us do all we can for her, or our prayer will be a mockery.

C.  Let us do nothing to grieve the Lord; for all depends upon His smile. "Cause Thy face to shine."

D.  Let us pray much more than we have done. Let each one of us be a Daniel.

- During the troublous times of Scotland, when the royal court and aristocracy were arming themselves to suppress the Reformation in that land, and the cause of Protestant Christianity was in imminent peril, late on a certain night John Knox was seen to leave his study, and to pass from the house down into an enclosure to the rear of it.

  He was followed by a friend, when, after a few moments of silence, his voice was heard as if in prayer. In another moment the accents deepened into intelligible words, and the current petition went up from his struggling soul to heaven, "O Lord, give me Scotland, or I die!" Then a pause of hushed stillness, when again the petition broke forth, "O Lord, give me Scotland, or I die!"

  Once more all was voiceless and noiseless, when, with a yet intenser pathos the thrice-repeated intercession struggled forth, "O Lord, give me Scotland, or I die!" And God gave him Scotland in spite of Mary and her Cardinal Beaton; a land and a church of noble loyalty to Christ and His crown.

  The church may be sick, yet not die. Die it cannot, for the blood of an eternal King bought it, the power of an eternal Spirit preserves it, and the mercy of an eternal God shall crown it.                                              —Thomas Adams.

CONDENSED FROM C. H. SPURGEON

# PRAYER FOUND IN THE HEART

*"For Thou, O Lord of hosts, God of Israel, has revealed
to Thy servant, saying, I will build thee an house: therefore
hath Thy servant found in his heart to pray this prayer
unto Thee" (2 Sam. 7:27).*

How often God does for His servants what they desire to do for
Him! David desired to build the Lord a house, and the Lord built
*him* a house.

I.  How Did He Come by His Prayer? He "found in his heart
to pray this prayer."

He found it, which is a sign he looked for it. Those who pray
at random will never be accepted; we must carefully seek out our
prayers (Job 13:4).

In his heart—not in a book, nor in his memory, nor in his
head, nor in his imagination, nor only on his tongue (Ps. 84:2).

It is proof that he had a heart, knew where it was, could look
into it, and did often search it (Ps. 67:6).

It must have been a living heart, or a living prayer would not
have been within it.

It must have been a believing heart, or he would not have
found "this prayer" in it.

It must have been a serious heart, not flippant, forgetful,
cold, indifferent, or he would have found a thousand vanities in it,
but no prayer. Question: Would prayer be found in your heart at
this time? (Hos. 7:11).

II.  How Did This Prayer Come to Be in His Heart?

A.  The Lord's own Spirit instructed him how to pray. By
giving him a sense of need. Great blessings teach us our necessity,
as in David's case.

B.  The Lord inclined him to pray.

It has been said that an absolute promise would render
prayer needless; whereas the first influence of such a promise is to
suggest prayer. The Lord inclined David's heart by warming his
heart. Prayer does not grow in an icebox.

III.  How May You Find Prayer in Your Hearts?

Look into your heart, and make diligent search.

Think of your own need, and this will suggest petitions.

Think of your situation, and you will humbly cry to the Lord.

Think of the promises, the precepts, and the doctrines of truth, and each one of these will summon you to your knees.

Have Christ in your heart, and prayer will follow (Acts 9:11).

Live near to God, and then you will often speak to Him.

Do you find prayers and other holy things in your heart? Or is it full of vanity, worldliness, ambition, and ungodliness?

Remember that you are what your heart is (Prov. 23:7).

- "A great part of my time," said M'Cheyne, "is spent in getting my heart in tune for prayer."

    It is not the gilded paper and good writing of a petition that prevails with a king, but the moving sense of it. And to that King who discerns the heart, heart-sense is the sense of all, and that which He only regards; He listens to hear what that speaks, and takes all as nothing where that is silent. All other excellence in prayer is but the outside and fashion of it; this is the life of it.                                    —Leighton.

- I asked a young friend, "Did you pray before conversion?" She answered that she did after a sort. I then inquired, "What is the difference between your present prayers and those before you knew the Lord?" Her answer was, "Then I said my prayers, but now I *mean* them. Then I said the prayers which other people taught me, but now I find them in my heart."

    There is good reason to cry "Eureka!" when we find prayer in our heart. Holy Bradford would never cease praying or praising till he found his heart thoroughly engaged in the holy exercise. If it be not in my heart to pray, I must pray till it is. But oh, the delight of pleading with God when the heart casts forth mighty jets of supplication, like a geyser in full action! How mighty is supplication when the whole soul becomes one living, hungering, expecting desire!

    Remember, God respects not the arithmetic of our prayers, how many they are; nor the rhetoric of our prayers, how long they are; nor the music of our prayers, how methodical they are; but the divinity of our prayers, how heart-sprung they are. Not gifts, but graces, prevail in prayer.                  —Trapp.

CONDENSED FROM C. H. SPURGEON

# THE PRAYER GOD WILL NOT DESPISE

*"He will regard the prayer of the destitute, and
not despise their prayer" (Ps. 100:17).*

No religion without prayer. All pagan religions have it.
Mohammedanism abounds in it. Scenes I have witnessed of it. The
sound from the minarets, calling the believers to prayer several
times a day. Jews under the law were distinguished for prayer—
Christianity is saturated with the spirit of prayer. Directions, cautions
and promises we have in every conceivable form. The text contains
two distinct declarations in reference to prayer. Let us look at these
two declarations in their various bearings.

I.  **God Will Not Despise Their Prayer.**
   To despise is to scorn, to condemn. The declaration obviously
involves the truth that there are prayers God will despise. Our subject,
therefore, will be best discussed by looking at such prayers as God
despises, that is, treats with His Divine scorn; and,
   A.  He will *despise* prayers that *seek* to do *evil*. Malicious
prayers, vengeful prayers. Prayer must be without wrath. Such prayers
are in reality seeking to hurt others.
   B.  He will *despise* the prayers of mere *terror*. Wicked
profane persons, when in danger only, pray. Often sailors in storms—
soldiers in battle—persons in sudden peril (see Prov. 1:23).
   C.  He will *despise* all *ostentatious* prayers. Mere parade of
piety, learning, or display of gifts, or show of goodness (Matt. 6:5;
13:5, etc.).
   D.  He will *despise* merely *long* prayers (Matt. 23:14). So
Christ's Divine model is in a few sentences.
   E.  He will *despise* all mere *wordy* prayers. Just prattling to
God—prayers with a bushel of words to a few ideas—vague, diffuse,
verbose.
   F.  He will *despise* all *arrogant* prayers. Teaching God, or
preaching to God, explaining to God as if He did not understand, or
in prayer preaching to those who hear us, or dictating and telling
God what He ought to do.
   G.  He will *despise* all *uncharitable* prayers. Prayer can only
rise on the wings of love. Hear Christ (Matt. 5:23).

H. He will *despise* all *unbelieving* prayers. "He that cometh to God must believe," etc. Faith essential—without it prayer is mockery, contradiction, absurdity. It may be weak faith, but faith is essential.

I. He will *despise* all *ungrateful* prayers. Prayer and thanksgiving must be the two links of acceptable devotion. Make your request with thanksgiving (1 Thess. 5:17).

J. He will *despise* all *self-meritorious* prayers. Resting on our supposed excellency or merit—leaving out the Mediator and His work, etc.

K. He will *despise* all *presumptuous* prayers. Where we ask God to do for us what we can do ourselves, or ask what involves a miracle, or for personal convenience, without regard to others, or God's general providence and His government of the world. To pray for removal of epidemics and dwelling in dirt.

L. He will *despise* the *insincere* prayer. Mere lip devotion—nominal dead form. Now these must be our beacon lights when we pray. But the text refers to,

II. The Prayer He Will Not Despise.

"The prayers of the destitute."

A. Who feel their need.

B. Who realize their dependence on Him.

C. Who acknowledge their sins and unworthiness. Publican, etc.

D. Who press their case. Woman of Canaan, etc.

E. Who honor His Word by confidence and persistency. Will not let thee go, etc.

F. Who ignore themselves. Deep in the valley.

G. Who pray in Christ's name, etc.

Application

1. How condescending God is. To the poorest, most wretched, forlorn, widow, orphan, beggar, etc.
2. How good God is to all.
3. How all-sufficient God is to His people.
4. How we should learn to pray and seek His grace.

JABEZ BURNS

# PRAYER: ITS OUGHTNESS

*"Men ought always to pray" (Luke 18:1).*

In a prominent place in the *Chicago Tribune* appeared the following:

"Prayer Before Meals an Aid to Digestion.

"Philadelphia, PA., June 28—In addition to being an excellent religious practice, the saying of grace before meals is an aid to digestion, Dr. Gilbert Fitzpatrick, of Chicago, president of the American Institute of Homeopathy, told the eighty-second annual convention of the institute.

"Family squabbles, business problems, and other frictional disturbances tend to disrupt the process of digestion, Dr. Fitzpatrick added. Instead, he advocated laughter and cheer at meal-time."

There are many reasons why we should pray. The following are some of them:

I.   The Behest of Prayer.
The commands of the Lord are for our obedience; hence, we are to "pray without ceasing" (1 Thess. 5:17).

II.   The Benefit of Prayer.
The teaching of the parable is, God will undertake our cause if we plead with importunity (Luke 18:7).

III.   The Brotherliness of Prayer.
"Epaphras . . . laboring fervently in prayer" (Col. 4:12). There is no ministry so effective in helping others like prayer.

IV.   The Benediction of Prayer.
When prayer is coupled with thanksgiving and carefulness about nothing, it bestows the benediction of the peace of God (Phil. 4:6,7).

V.   The Betterment of Prayer.
No one can truly pray without being the better for it, for coming to God, we are receivers from Him, for we become like that which we receive. The disciples received the Spirit in answer to prayer, and that caused a marked difference in their lives (Acts 1:14; 2:1-4).

F. E. MARSH

# PRAYER: ITS PRIVILEGE AND POWER

*"In prayer" (Neh. 11:17).*

Dr. Rendle Harris, in *The Guiding Hand of God*, tells of a father in Oxford who was caused one evening to pray for his soldier son, absent on service in the South African War. Under the same impelling, he continued in prayer till the morning broke. Then came relief, and he went to rest. It transpired that in the distant land his son had been brought very seriously wounded into the hospital. The doctor had at first declared there to be no hope, but yielding to the nurse's pleading, they had together fought through the night to save that life, and at dawn the crisis had been passed. It was in the "self-same hour" that this father had felt that he could cease his intercession. Prayer, when it becomes a reality, opens the eyes and directs the gaze upon the unseen. The secrets of the Lord are ours.

Several times we find the words "In prayer."

I.  Articulated Prayer.—"Whiles I was speaking *In Prayer*" (Dan. 9:21).

II. Privileged Prayer.—"Whatsoever ye shall ask *In Prayer*" (Matt. 21:22).

III. Continued Prayer.—"Continued all night *In Prayer*" (Luke 6:12).

IV. United Prayer.—"One accord *In Prayer* and supplication" (Acts 1:14).

V.  Exampled Prayer.—"Labored fervently *In Prayers*" (Col. 4:12).

VI. Intense Prayer.—"Continuing *In Prayer*" (Rom. 12:12).

VII. Watchful Prayer.—"Continue *In Prayer*, and watch in the same" (Col. 4:2).

F. E. MARSH

- Mrs. Billy Graham once told an audience of Minneapolis women: "God has not always answered my prayers. If He had, I would have married the wrong man—several times."

RELIGIOUS NEW SERVICE

# PRAYER: JACOB WRESTLING WITH THE ANGEL

*"And Jacob was left alone; and there wrestled a man with him until the break of day. And when he saw that he prevailed not against him, he touched the hollow of his thigh; and the hollow of Jacob's thigh was out of joint, as he wrestled with him" (Gen. 32:24,25, etc.)*

The patriarchs and early saints possessed not the valuable direction of a written revelation. In that early age there were none especially inspired either to teach or prophesy to the people. To make up for this, God often revealed Himself to His saints, especially by visions and dreams of the night. Oftentimes too Jehovah appeared to discourse with them, assuming sometimes the form of a man, and at other times the appearance of an angel. Jacob was favored with two of these special manifestations. At Bethel, where he saw the ladder reaching to heaven, and on this occasion.

    I.   The Circumstances in Which Jacob Was Placed.

    II.  His Mysterious Conflict.

    III.  His Wondrous Victory.

    IV.  The Blessings Which Followed.

### I.  The Circumstances in Which He Was Placed.

A.  *He was returning into his own country.* He left it through fear of his angry brother. More than twenty years had passed. His return was under God's direction (v. 9). "In all thy ways acknowledge," etc. "Commit thy way," etc.

B.  *His brother was announced as coming in wrath to meet him.* He had wisely and piously sent a message of kindness to Esau (v. 3, etc.); but his resentment was aroused, and Jacob is informed of his hostility, etc. (v. 6).

C.  *He had prudently arranged his temporal concerns.* His peril seemed awfully imminent. What could he do (v. 7)?

D.  *He had fervently poured out his soul to God.* He followed up all with earnest prayer. He pleaded God's promises (vv. 9 to 12). Having done this, he sent ahead his flocks, and also his family.

E.  *He was now enjoying devotional solitude.* "Alone," so far as mortal beings were concerned. "Alone," to plead his cause with God. "Alone," to confess his sins, and to open all his heart to the Lord.

### II.  His Mysterious Conflict.
This conflict was mysterious indeed; we have nothing like it on record. It was not merely mental.

His body and soul were engaged; but who was the glorious being, etc. "A man," says the text; but in verse 28, he is said to have "power with God" (see Hos. 12:4,5). None other than Jehovah Jesus. God in the appearance of humanity. God anticipating His incarnation, etc.

A.  How unequal the conflict!

B.  How protracted! lasted for several hours.

C.  To show the weakness of Jacob, and his own power, he touches him and disjoints the hollow of his thigh; but still Jacob maintains the struggle.

D.  He solicits permission to retire. "Let me go, for the day breaketh." How easily he could have done so! but he honors Jacob's perseverance, and elicits his strongest faith. God will not oppose physical might to moral power. He allows moral influence to prevail.

E.  Notice, Jacob resolves not to yield without the blessing. "I will not," etc. What valor, perseverance! And now observe,

III.  **The Wondrous Victory He Achieved.** God allows omnipotence to yield to the influence of faithful prayer. In token of the victory,

A.  He obliterates his former name. No more Jacob (i.e., Supplanter), the sins and frailties of the past blotted out (see chapter 27:34, etc.).

B.  A new name is given, "Israel," a name of honor and holy distinction. "One who has power with Jehovah." The title was one of great honor, and everlasting renown; a name, too, which should descend to thousands of thousands, and to generations then unborn. Then notice,

IV.  **The Blessings Which Followed** (v. 23). "And with men," etc. This victory was the assurance that men should not overcome or destroy him, the less victory would certainly follow the greater.

A.  The mind of Jacob was filled with sublime yet sweet conceptions of God's glory. He called the place, "Peniel," etc.

B.  He marveled at his own preservation. "And my life is preserved."

C.  The wrath of his brother was turned aside. His heart was in the Lord's hand, and he subdued and softened it. "If a man's ways please the Lord," etc.

D.   He retained, however, the sense of his weakness. "He halted upon his thigh." Lest he should be exalted above measure. To keep him prostrate before the Lord, etc.

### Application

1.   *The marvelous potency of prayer*. How wondrous its achievements! What has it wrought?

2.   *The secret of its power is fervor*. Persevering fervor. What was symbolized by Jacob's wrestling? Not fainting; not ceasing; but pleading, and pressing our case. Let us long for, and seek the spirit of prayer, and the grace of supplication.

3.   *Let the prayerless now see the value of prayer*.

JABEZ BURNS

---

## PRAYER OF FAITH

---

  I.   Confession of sin.
"To seek by prayer and supplication" (Dan. 9:3-20).

 II.   Cleansing from sin.
"Thy sin purged" (Isa. 6:7).

III.   Consecration to the Savior.
"Behold, he prayeth" (Acts 9:11-20).

IV.   Confidence in the Savior.
"Said unto the Lord, increase our faith" (Luke 17:5).

 V.   Courage from the Savior.
"They lifted up their voice to God with one accord" (Acts 4:24-33).

VI.   Calmness in the Savior.
"The peace of God . . . . shall keep your hearts and minds" (Phil. 4:6,7).

VII.   Communion with the Savior.
"Did not our heart burn . . . while He talked with us" (Luke 24:32).

F. E. MARSH

---

# PRAYER: RICHARD BAXTER'S TESTIMONY

*"Whatsoever ye shall ask" (Matt. 21:22).*

Richard Baxter has left this testimony: "Many a time when I have been brought low, and received the sentence of death in myself, when my poor, honest, and praying neighbors have met, and, upon their fasting and earnest prayers I have recovered. Once, when I had continued weak three weeks, and was unable to go abroad, the very day they prayed for me, being Good Friday, I recovered, and was able to preach, and administer the sacrament the next Lord's day; and was better after it, it being the first time I ever administered it. And ever after that, whatever weakness was upon me, when I had, after preaching, administered the sacrament to many hundreds of people, I was much revived and eased of my infirmities."

If we ask rightly, we shall obtain bountifully. If we ask wrongly, we shall obtain disastrously.

### I. Asking in Prayer.

"Ask and it shall be given you" (Matt. 7:7-11). Have something to ask for, and get what you ask, then the benefit of asking will be enjoyed.

### II. Asking for Help.

"Give to every man that asketh of thee" (Luke 6:30). Better to make mistakes in giving, than to have the mistakes of an ungenerous nature.

### III. Asking for Water.

"Askest drink of Me." " . . . Thou wouldest have asked of Him" (John 4:9,10). Water from earth's resources fails, but Christ's reservoir is lasting and satisfying.

### IV. Asking for Light.

The jailer "called (asked) for a light" (Acts 16:29). He needed light in a twofold sense. To see how things were, and to see his spiritual need.

### V. Asking for Wisdom.

"If any man lack wisdom, let him ask of God" (James 1:5). To be wise through God's Word is to have a wisdom worth having.

### VI. Asking for Filling.

Paul's "desire" (same word as "ask"—$\alpha\iota\tau\epsilon\omega$, Col. 1:9) for the saints of Colosse was that they might be "filled" with the knowledge of God's will.

VII.   Asking for a Murderer.

The people were incited to "ask" for Barabbas, and their sad choice is recorded against them (Matt. 27:20; Acts 3:14).

F. E. MARSH

## THE PRAYER OF THE PENITENT

*"Have mercy upon me, O God," etc. (Ps. 51:1,2).*

A great saint expressing great sorrow for great sin.

 I.   The Penitent's Prayer.
   A.   It was a public prayer. "To the chief musician."
   B.   It was a prayer for pity.
   Three ways of treating sin: indifference, severity, mercy.
The third is God's way, as revealed specially by Christ.
   C.   It was a prayer for pardon.
   Sin must be blotted out before peace can be restored.
   D.   It was a prayer for purification.
   "Wash me *thoroughly*."
   E.   In this prayer there is a recognition of his:
      1.   Perilous position.
      2.   Personal accountability: *"my* sin."

 II.   The Penitent's Plea.
   He does not plead:
   His past purity.
   His pious parentage.
   His public position.
   His princely prowess.

He pleads:

The plenitude of God's mercy. A *multitude* of tender mercies!

SELECTED

# A PRAYER SUITED TO ALL

*"O remember not against us former iniquities; let Thy tender mercies speedily prevent us; for we are brought very low" (Ps. 79:8).*

*"Do not hold against us the sins of the fathers; may Your mercy come quickly to meet us, for we are in desperate need" (Ps. 79:8 NIV).*

We may all use this prayer, and on some occasions it may be more than ordinarily appropriate. Its admissions—its earnest entreaties—and its appeal, may most profitably be copied.

Notice,

## I. What Is Deprecated.

"God's remembrance of former iniquities." Now three thoughts are here suggested. We are conscious:

A.  Of our *iniquities*. Crooked, perverse, evil ways and doings; a foul blot on our life's record; an evil stain on our consciences; and terribly wicked before God.

Observe,

B.  The *continuity* of our *iniquities*. We might divide them into many kinds and degrees, but the word "former" reminds us of those in earlier life—iniquities of youth and of early manhood, or of past days. There are later and more recent iniquities, and they are all to be confessed before God. "I will acknowledge mine iniquity," etc.

C.  He *seeks* that God will *not remember* these *"iniquities."* God's perfect and infinite knowledge renders it impossible for Him to forget anything, but while this is so, He has said, in reference to His true repentant people, He will remember their iniquities no more. He will not charge the people with their sins, or punish the people on account of them. So this is what is sought in the text. God might both remember and punish them. His holiness and justice would seem to demand it.

Notice,

## II. The Plea He Presents on This Account.

God's tender mercies. "Let Thy tender mercies speedily prevent us." The Amplified Bible reads: "Let Your compassion and tender mercies speedily come to meet us. . . ." See this plea in its various parts:

A.  God's *mercies*. Not *mercy*, but *mercies*—adapted to all sorts of iniquities. These mercies are the overflowing of goodness, love, compassion, pity, etc. They are even of old, flow in varied forms, are everlasting, universal over all God's works.

B. *Tender mercies*. As the father's mercies toward his children—as the soft gushings forth of the loving mother. In themselves tender, in their manifestation tender, etc. Father and prodigal—Jesus and woman sinner. He asks that these iniquities may be prevented by His "tender mercies."

C. *Go before*, or *prevent* us. Prevent our arrestment, trial, penalty, misery and ruin.

D. *Speedily*. For our anxiety is extreme—our conviction deep—anguish great—forebodings terrible. We are perishing, therefore "speedily," etc.

See,

## II. The Humble Admission.

"For we are brought very low." Low—

A. In our *sinful degradation*. As the prodigal. Low—

B. In our *moral weakness*. Moral vigor gone—righteous strength exhausted. As wasted by disease helpless, etc. But low also,

C. In our *sense of wretchedness*. Without joy or peace or comfort. As in the mire and clay—as in a gloomy prison—as close to the yawning gulf—yet not too low to cry for help and implore mercy.

## Application

Our subject is one:

1. Of personal importance. That we should all individually realize it.

2. How often applicable to families and households. Jacob's, Eli's, David's, etc.

3. It may be appropriate to churches (see Rev. 2, 3).

4. Or to nations. How clear, direct and simple is the spirit of the text. Let all labor to feel and then express the prayer.

JABEZ BURNS

## PRAYER: THE GREATEST MINISTRY OF ALL

*"Ye also helping together by prayer for us" (2 Cor. 1:11).*

A station in the China Inland Mission was peculiarly blessed of God. Inquirers were more numerous and more easily turned from dumb idols to serve the living God than at other stations. The difference was a theme of conversation and wonder.

In England Dr. J. Hudson Taylor was warmly greeted at a certain place by a stranger who showed great interest in his mission work. He was so particular and intelligent in his questions concerning one missionary and the locality in which he labored, and seemed so well acquainted with his helpers, inquirers, and the difficulties of that particular station, that Dr. Taylor's curiosity was aroused to find out the reason for this intimate knowledge. He now learned that this stranger and the successful missionary had covenanted together as co-workers. The missionary kept his home brother informed of all the phases of his labor. He gave him the names of inquirers, stations, hopeful characters and difficulties, and all these the home worker made it a practice to spread out before God in prevailing prayer.

There is no ministry so effective and helpful as the intercession of prayer. Think of some of the results as brought out in the Book of Acts.

I. Prayer brought the *Power of Pentecost* (Acts 2:4).

II. Prayer brought *Renewed Grace* to the disciples in need (Acts 4:31).

III. Prayer brought *Discretion* and *Direction* to the early church in missionary work (Acts 13:3).

IV. Prayer *Sustained* Paul and Silas in suffering and persecution, and made them a blessing to others (Acts 16:25).

V. Prayer *Brought Peter Out of Prison* by means of angelic ministry (Acts 12:5).

VI. Prayer brought *Consolation* to the church in Ephesus, when Paul left it (Acts 20:36).

VII. Prayer brought *Help* to Saul of Tarsus in his need (Acts 9:11).

F. E. MARSH

# PRAYER: THREE KINDS

*"Master, have mercy upon us! . . . Where are the nine?" (Luke 17:13, 17).*
*"Pharisee . . . prayed with himself" (Luke 18:11).*
*"God be merciful to me a sinner" (Luke 18:13).*

Bishop Jeremy Taylor has described three kinds of prayers:

> "Many, in direst trouble, pray;
> But when that trouble's over they
> Forget to give the praise that's due
> To the good God who helped them through.
> "Some, like the Pharisee, oft pray
> Thus with themselves, thankful that they
> Are not so bad as those 'than whom
> I thank Thee that I better am.'
> 'Better in what? That thou'rt a sham?
> Wouldst thou do better in their room?'
> "But, like the publican, I'd rather
> Beat on my breast, and cry, 'Oh! Father,
> A sinner I; have mercy, Thou!
> From my worse self, oh, save me now!'"

### I. Praise-less Prayers.

Thankless ones like the lepers, who did not return to thank the Lord. Those who are wanting in praise will be wanting in blessing.

### II. Pharisaical Prayers.

The Pharisee prayed "with himself," about himself, but not *for* himself. His prayer began, continued, and ended in himself.

> "I, I, I, I, itself;
> The inside and the outside,
> The what and the why,
> The when and the where,
> The low and the high,
> All I, I, I, I, itself I."

### III. Publican's Prayer.

His prayer was for mercy, because he knew he was a sinner; what he actually prayed was, "God be favorably inclined to me, the sinner" (Luke 18:13), or as it might be rendered, "God make an atonement for me, the sinner." The word "merciful" is translated "make reconciliation" in the Revised Version of Hebrews 2:17. It reads, "Make propitiation" (atonement) "for the sins of the people," and refers to the high priest on the Day of Atonement, in his making an atonement for the sins of the people (see Lev. 16).

F. E. MARSH

# PRAYER OF FAITH

*"The prayer of faith" (James 5:15).*

There are many things which are said to be "of faith." There is the "walk of faith" which companions with the company of God (2 Cor. 5:7); there is "the Word of faith" which listens to the voice of God (Rom. 10:8); and there is "the prayer of faith" which hands everything over to God (James 5:15).

The word "prayer" in the sentence "the prayer of faith," is peculiar in its inwardness. It indicates the inner condition of the one who prays.

There are only two other instances where the same word is rendered "prayer." Once when it says of Christ, "He prayed," and the other place where we read, "They prayed and fasted" (Luke 9:29; Acts 13:1-3). Wrapped up in the soul of the word there is implied the faithfulness of a consistent life in the one who prays, therefore no one prays "the prayer of faith" who does not live in the life of faithfulness. Burns happily expresses the thought in the *Cotter's Saturday Night*, when he says,

"They never sought in vain,
Who sought the Lord aright."
The Prayer of Faith is:

  I. **Secret in Its Fellowship.** "When thou prayest, enter into thy closet . . . pray to thy Father which is in secret" (Matt. 6:6).

 II. **Submissive in Its Attitude.** Christ prayed saying, "Thy will be done" (Matt. 26:42, 44).

III. **Supplicating in Its Service.** "Prayed for them" (Acts 8:15).

 IV. **Sincere in Its Request.** "I prayed in mine house" (Acts 10:30).

  V. **Sanctified in Its Desire.** "When they had fasted and prayed" (Acts 13:3).

 VI. **Symphonizing with Others.** "If two of you shall agree on earth, as touching anything that they shall ask, it shall be done for them of My Father which is in heaven" (Matt. 18:19).

VII. **Single-Hearted in Its Devotion.** "We made our prayer unto God" (Neh. 4:9).

F. E. MARSH

# PREVAILING PRAYER

*Genesis 32*

### I. Prevailing Prayer Pleads the Promises (v. 9).

Trapp says: "Promises must be prayed over. God loves to be burdened with, and to be importuned in His own words; to be sued upon His own bond. Prayer is putting the promises into suit. Such prayers will be nigh the Lord day and night (1 Kings 8:59). He can as little deny them as deny Himself."

### II. Prevailing Prayer Confesses Its Unworthiness (v. 10).

We do not receive blessing because of our confession, but we are not blest without it.

### III. Prevailing Prayer Asks Definitely (v. 11).

Jacob knew what he wanted, and prayed accordingly. He had offended and robbed his brother, and now he seeks deliverance from his righteous anger. The Lord often overrules our blunders to our benefit and His own glory. Jacob not only prays for himself, but also for those who are near and dear to him.

### IV. Prevailing Prayer Is to Be Alone with God (v. 24).

The words of Christ are "Pray in secret" (Matt. 6:6). Christ is our Example in this, for He went to the mountain to pray (Matt. 14:23). Praying in secret we will get revelations of His glory, as Daniel did at the riverside (Dan. 8:16); we will have the consciousness of the presence of Christ, as John had on the Isle of Patmos (Rev. 1); we will be commissioned, as Peter was, when he was on the housetop at Joppa (Acts. 10:9); we will meet the Rebekahs of blessing, as Isaac did, when meditating in the field (Gen. 24:63); and we will receive blessing, as Jacob did.

### V. Prevailing Prayer Is Intensely Earnest.

Trapp well remarks, in speaking of the angel wrestling with Jacob: "There wrestled a man with him; in a proper combat, by might and sleight; to the raising of dust and causing of sweat, as the word importeth. This strife was not only corporeal, but spiritual; as well as by the force of his faith, as strength of body. 'He prevaileth,' saith the prophet (Hos. 12:4), by prayers and tears. Our Savior also prayed Himself into 'an agony' (Luke 22:44); and we are bidden to 'strive in prayer' (Rom. 15:30); Nehemiah prayed himself pale (Neh.

2:2); Daniel prayed himself 'sick' (Dan. 8:27). Hannah prayed, striving with such an unusual motion of her lips, that old Eli, looking upon her, thought her drunk (1 Sam. 1:13). Elijah put his head between his knees, as straining every spring of heart in prayer (1 Kings 18:42). Every sound is not music, so neither is every uttering of petitions to God a prayer. It is not the labor of the lips, but the travail of the heart. Common beggary is the easiest and poorest trade; but this beggary, as it is the richest so it is the hardest."

**VI. Prevailing Prayer Is Seen in a Clinging Faith** (v. 26).

Jacob got no blessing while wrestling, but the wrestling led to the blessing. The angel touched his thigh, and then he could wrestle no more, but he held on the tighter, and would not let the angel go till he received a blessing from him. Three boys each gave a definition of faith, which definitions illustrate the tenacity of faith. The first boy said, "It was taking hold of Christ"; the second, "Keeping hold"; and the third, "not letting go."

**VII. Prevailing Prayer Is Rewarded** (vv. 28-30).

   A.  He got his name changed from Jacob, the supplanter, to Israel, the prince of God.

   B.  He received definite blessing from God.

   C.  He was a testimony for God ever afterwards in his halting gait.

F. E. MARSH


## SEVEN FACTS ABOUT PRAYER

*Eph. 6:18-19*

   I.   The Season of prayer. "Always."

   II.  The Way of prayer. "With all prayer and supplication."

   III. The Subject of prayer. "For all saints."

   IV.  The Power of prayer. "In the Spirit."

   V.   The Continuance of prayer. "With all perseverance."

   VI.  The Individuality of prayer. "And for me" (v. 19).

   VII. The Subject of prayer. "That I may speak boldly" (v. 19).

INGLIS

# PRINCIPLES OF PRAYER

*"They tell him of her" (Mark 1:30).*

"They tell Him of her." How simple and yet how striking the words! In them are found the essential and essence of prayer. Emphasize each word.

"*They* tell Him of her." The men who are in touch with Christ have the ear of Christ. Holy John, zealous Peter, discriminating James, and faithful Andrew, are the men who are in touch with Christ. These men in their several characteristics may be taken as illustrating four essentials in prayer, namely, holiness, zeal, discrimination and faithfulness.

## I. *Holiness* of the heart and life are the *foundation of prayer.*

It is no use lifting up our hands if they are not holy (1 Tim. 2:8); nor must we approach the golden altar of incense to offer praise before we have washed away the filthiness of flesh and spirit at the laver of God's truth by confession (2 Cor. 7:1).

## II. *Fervency* of spirit is the *prevailer of prayer.*

It was the importunate widow who got her plea granted (Luke 18:5); it was the persistent friend who got his need supplied (Luke 11:8); and it was the incessant knocking of Peter which caused the inmates to let him into the house (Acts 12:16).

## III. *Discrimination* is the *wisdom of prayer.*

There are some things for which God's people ask, that they have already received in Christ; others are praying when they should be acting, asking God to do things which they can do themselves; and others are praying in a wrong spirit. To discriminate in prayer is to observe the conditions for prevailing in prayer.

## IV. *Faithfulness* is the *backbone of prayer.*

Faithfulness may be read two ways. First, consistency or fidelity to the Word of God in wholehearted obedience; and second, fullness of faith, that is, an unhesitating and unceasing confidence and trust in God.

"They *tell* Him of her." What is prayer? It is illustrated here. Speaking to Christ is prayer. Prayer is not getting on to the stilts of wordism, nor floating in the balloon of honeyed phrases by the aid of the gas of human eloquence, inflating the mind with self-conceit; but it is simply telling the Lord the heart's need, or speaking to Him in a natural manner as we ask favors for others.

Telling Him the *trouble*, as the disciples of John, when they went and informed Christ that their teacher was beheaded (Matt. 14:12).

Telling Him the *sorrow*, as when Mary went to Christ about her dead brother Lazarus (John 11:32).

Telling Him the *pain*, as when Paul prayed about the thorn in the flesh (2 Cor. 12:8).

Telling Him the *grief*, as when the Syrophoenician woman cried to Christ about her daughter (Matt. 15:22).

Telling Him the *joy*, as when the disciples spoke of the demons they had cast out in His name (Luke 10:17).

Telling Him the *difficulty*, as when the disciples asked to be taught how to pray (Luke 11:1).

Telling Him the *sickness*, as in the present case.

"They tell *Him* of her." There is no need to mention *His* name, we have only to put a capital H to the pronoun for it to be recognized that we speak of Christ. He has made it possible for us to tell Him, for He has died for us; hence we can come boldly to the throne of grace through the consecrated way of His atonement, and speak to Him face to face. He has told us to come to Him, for He has said, "Whatsoever we shall ask in prayer, believing, we shall receive." His promise is our plea and introduction in speaking to Him. We remember who He is, and as we do so we are drawn toward Him, as the needle is drawn to the magnet.

He is the *Shepherd* who tends us, and ever looks after our interests.

He is the *Priest* who represents us, and helps us in the hour of temptation.

He is the *Friend* who thinks of us, and always sympathizes with us.

He is the *Brother* who cares for us, and is ever ready to aid us.

He is the *Savior* who delivered us, and will always keep us.

He is the *God* who has blessed us, and will never leave us.

He is the *Lover* who loves us, and will never be unfaithful.

Tell Him, for He *cares*. Tell Him, for He *knows*. Tell Him, for He *loves*. Tell Him, for He is *listening*. Tell Him *all*. Tell Him *often*. Tell Him *always*. Tell Him *now*.

"They tell Him of *her*." They were very definite in their petition and pointed in their plea. They did not vacillate or hesitate, but they went right to the mark and hit it. And as they saw the once fevered patient calm and cool, as she waited upon them, they rejoiced; and if they had wanted a new name for Simon's wife's mother, they might have called her Answered-Prayer.                    F. E. MARSH

# THE SECRET OF SUCCESSFUL PRAYER

I. **Faith.**

Ask in faith, nothing wavering (James 1:6).

Believe that ye receive, and ye shall have (Mark 11:24).

Whatsoever ye shall ask in prayer, believing, ye shall receive (Matt. 21:22).

According to your faith be it unto you (Matt. 9:29).

As thou hast believed, so be it done unto thee (Matt. 8:13).

The prayer of faith shall save the sick (James 5:18).

II. **In the Name of Jesus.**

Whatsoever ye shall ask in My name, that will I do (John 14:13,14).

III. **Submission to God's Will.**

If we ask anything according to His will, He heareth us (1 John 5:14).

IV. **Obedience.**

Whatsoever we ask we receive of Him, because we keep His commandments (1 John 3:22).

The effectual fervent prayer of a righteous man availeth much (James 5:17).

The prayer of the upright is His delight (Prov. 15:8).

He heareth the prayer of the righteous (Prov. 15:29).

If any man doeth His will, him He heareth (John 9:13).

Contrast: If I regard iniquity in my heart, the Lord will not hear me (Ps. 66:18).

V. **Sincerity.**

The Lord is nigh unto all them that call upon Him in truth (Ps. 145:18).

Let us draw near with a true heart (Heb. 10:22).

Use not vain repetitions (Matt. 6:7).

VI. **Boldness and Confidence.**

Ask, and it shall be given you (Matt. 7:7).

Let us come boldly . . . that we may obtain (Heb. 4:16).

Having boldness . . . let us draw near in full assurance (Heb. 10:19, 22).

VII. Humility.

If My people will humble themselves . . . then will I hear (2 Chron. 7:14).

He forgetteth not the cry of the humble (Ps. 9:12).

Thou hast heard the desire of the humble (Ps. 10:17).

VIII. Abiding and Delighting in God.

If ye abide in Me . . . ye shall ask what ye will, and it shall be done (John 15:7).

Delight thyself in the Lord, and He shall give thee the desires of thy heart (Ps. 37:4).

IX. Union with Others in Prayer.

If two of you shall agree . . . it shall be done for them (Matt. 18:19).

FOOTSTEPS OF TRUTH

## HOW SHOULD WE PRAY?

I. *Boldly* (Eph. 3:12; Heb. 4:16; 10:19,20).

II. *In faith* (Heb. 10:22; James 1:6).

III. *Without ceasing* (Luke 18:1; 21:36).

IV. *Constantly* (Eph. 6:18; Rom. 12:12).

V. *Earnestly* (Matt. 6:7; Isa. 55:6; 26:9).

VI. *Believingly* (Jer. 29:13).

VII. *In the name of Christ* (John 16:23, 26; 14:13).

VIII. *Expecting answers* (Mark 11:24).

IX. *In resignation to God's will* (Matt. 6:10).

X. *Reverently* (Ps. 89:7; Heb. 12:28).

XI. *In humility* (Ps. 10:17; Isa. 57:15).

XII. *And prayer will be answered* (John 14:13; 15:7; 16:24; Isa. 58:9; 65:24).

In believing faith let us "come boldly to the throne of grace, and pour out our hearts before Him," who waits to be gracious and to do for us "exceeding abundantly above all that we ask or think" (Eph. 3:20).

SELECTED

# A STUDY OF PRAYER

There are three lines along which we may study this subject, namely, the life, the laws, and the legacy of Prayer.

## I. The Life of Prayer Reflected in the Bible

Prayer *is* life. We are not only to say prayers but to become pray-ers, as Frances Havergal has said. Prayer is also an outlook, and an atmosphere, of which the Bible in all its parts is ample evidence.

To the great men and women who made this wonderful history, prayer was a life. It began in Eden when the sin of our first parents and God's grace toward them were brought home to their consciences. But just outside the gates we find an altar, to which, "at the end of days" (no doubt, the Sabbath, Gen. 4:3) Cain and Abel brought their offerings. In the same chapter (v. 26) we read, "Then began men to call upon the name of the Lord." In 5:22 and 6:9, we read that Enoch and Noah walked with God, a fellowship which implies an intense prayer-life.

This holy communion between man and God is more evident from the time of Abraham, whose track may be traced by the altars which he built. This is true also, in measure, of Isaac and Jacob. No one could live the life which Joseph did, except by dwelling in the secret place of the Most High and abiding under the shadow of the Almighty. The great souls of this long period of time are the men and women who were "friends of God," and were most at home in His company. No biblical life is more full of prayer than that of Moses. He and Samuel stand out from all others, in the Divine estimate, as men who had power and could prevail. The same could be said of Noah, Daniel, and Job (*cf.* Ezek. 14:14).

Not only by the prayers of Moses which are recorded, but from his whole story, we see how entirely his life was a life of prayer. Of praying kings should be named David, Solomon, and Asa, and Jehoshaphat, and Hezekiah, and Josiah. But for these men, and the prophets, the end of Judah had come much sooner; their prayers were the preserving salt in Israel.

Study the life and ministry of the prophets, and you will find that they were essentially men of prayer. But when we come to the New Testament fresh light falls upon the whole field of prayer, and new avenues of privileges are opened to us, new principles are revealed, and new possibilities of the prayer-life are disclosed. In the Old Testament prayer was occupied more especially with what is material and temporal, but in the New Testament more largely with what is moral and spiritual.

How sublime and strong a thing is the prayer-life in the New Testament. The example of our Lord is, of course, superlative. Collect all references in the Gospels which reflect this aspect of His life, and study the setting of each.

Christ's greatest Apostle was a man of prayer unceasing, and makes frequent reference to his intercessions and supplications. The Prayers of Paul constitute an ample subject for study, and much that is helpful has been written on them. James, also, urges the necessity of prayer; and the fragrance of John's own inner life is something that is felt in his books.

We should turn our attention next to:

## II. The Laws of Prayer Revealed in the Bible

The working of prayer is as definitely conditioned as the operations of nature, and we must know what these conditions are, and be subject to them if we would pray effectually. Prayer is not a leap in the dark, or a beating of the air, but a science in which cause and effect work with precision, and in which promise and performance have a fixed relation.

If we obey the precept, He will fulfill the promise; and until we do obey, let us cease to claim the promise.

To make prayer a substitute for performance is to violate one of its laws, and so to render it unavailing. I have heard of a domestic who asked her minister if he would pray for her that she might get up when the alarm rang in the morning; and he replied: "Certainly I will not; all you have to do is to put your feet on the floor."

Where desire and motive are carnal, prayer is not answered: "Ye ask and receive not, because ye ask amiss, that ye may consume it upon your lusts" (James 4:3).

Where the Divine will is set aside, prayer is not answered: "Ye shall cry out in that day because of your king which ye shall have chosen you; and the Lord will not hear you in that day" (1 Sam. 8:18).

Where there is unbelief, prayer is not answered: "He that wavereth is like a wave of the sea driven with the wind and tossed. Let not that man think that he shall receive anything of the Lord, a double minded man, unstable in all his ways" (James 1:8).

If we obey, God will operate; if we believe, He will bless; if we follow Him, He will fulfill His Word to us. Let us then come boldly to the throne of grace, which is the throne of the Divine government, and there prove Him, Who has permitted and bidden us so to do.

In closing, we may well think of:

### III.   The Legacy of Prayer Recorded in the Bible

Think, for example, of the colloquy of Abram and Jehovah over Sodom and Gomorrah (Gen. 18), and of Moses and Jehovah about the deliverance of Israel from Egyptian bondage (Ex. 3, 4); of David's song of praise in the day that the Lord delivered him out of the hands of all his enemies (2 Sam. 22); of Solomon's great prayer at the dedication of the Temple (1 Kings 8); of Daniel's confession, and Ezra's, and Nehemiah's, of the sins of their people in the ninth chapter of the books bearing their names. Think also, of Isaiah's earnest pleadings (63:7 to 64:12).

Coming to the New Testament, let us remember our Lord's great intercessory prayer (John 17); and the prayer which He taught His disciples (Matt. 6); and the prayers of Paul found in his Epistles to the Churches. If these were all we possessed we would be wealthy indeed, but we have innumerable smaller prayers scattered from Genesis to Revelation, prayers of Abram, and Lot, and Eliezer, and Isaac, and Jacob, and Job, and Moses, and Israel, and Joshua, and Gideon, and Samson, and Hannah, and Samuel, and David, and Korah, and Ethan, and Asaph, and Elijah, and Joel, and Jonah, and Amos, and Isaiah, and Hezekiah, and Habakkuk, and Nehemiah. And in the New Testament there are prayers of our Lord, and of His Apostles; of the martyred saints in the Apocalyptic vision; and of the redeemed and glorified in heaven. To this enormous heritage must be added numberless prayers of the saints of the Christian era from the first age of martyrdom down to the present day. When all this is considered, we shall be compelled to acknowledge that if we have failed in prayer, it has been largely due to ignorance or sloth. Let us arise and "possess our possessions."

CONDENSED FROM W. GRAHAM SCROGGIE

# UNAVAILING PRAYER

*"Thou hast covered thyself with a cloud, that our prayer should not pass through" (Lam. 3:44).*

The writer—the occasion—the griefs—patriotism—piety—zeal for God. How affecting these lamentations. Some of the thoughts are most tender. What bitter tears—what sad regrets (chap. 1:1-4; 2:10,11). So his personal experience (chap. 3:1-8). Now this verse is akin in spirit to the sentiment of the text. The day dawns (vv. 22, 31, etc.). But again sadness and wailing come out in our text. Notice,

### I. The Calamity Itself.

A "covered God"—"A thick cloud"—Prayer unable to penetrate. We do not wonder that God is thus,

    A. To the *incorrigible sinner*. Case stated (Prov. 1:28). Or to,

    B. The *miserable apostate* (Isa. 1:4-15; Jer. 11:10-11; Ezek. 8:17). Or to,

    C. *Nominal* and *unbelieving prayers*. This people draw, etc. "Ye have not," etc. (James 4:3). But see it in the case,

    D. Of *eminent saints* (Job 23:3-8). Paul (2 Cor. 12:8).

### II. The Sadness of This Calamity.

    A. *Spiritual darkness*. God unrecognized—Heaven hidden, with the sun's total eclipse.

    B. *Spiritual discomfort*. No light—way dark; mariner in night tempest. Paul's voyage (Acts 27).

    C. *Spiritual peril*. Darkness is danger. Wild beasts—bloody men.

    D. *Spiritual distressing apprehension*. Storm brooding—lightnings, etc.—forebodings of wrath, etc.

### III. The Occasions of This Calamity.

Not Divine eccentricity, pique or changeableness. The occasion is with man. It may arise from,

    A. Our *unfitness* for prayer. Worldly, selfish, earthly, angry, petulant, unloving, self-righteous.

    B. The *worthlessness* of our prayers. Formal, Pharisaic, cold, heartless, ungrateful.

    C. Our *spiritual state* not adapted for prayer. Frivolous, pleasure-takers, fashion seekers—fit for anything but devotion.

    D. *Unbelieving disobedience*. God has sought, asked, entreated—have we not often disregarded, refused, etc? Notice,

IV. The Remedy for This Sad Calamity.

A. *Unfeigned repentance* and *humiliation* before God. Words of confession—heart contrite—smitten breast, etc.

B. *Faith* in the Mediator. A day's-man is necessary—a Mediator—Advocate. Christ in His person, offices, work, righteousness, blood, etc.

C. The Spirit's *sanctifying power*—"helpeth our infirmities," etc.

D. Importance of *persistent supplication*. Jacob, Moses, Syrophoenician woman.

Application

1. To the prayerless. What a sad state.

2. To those experiencing the truth of the text. How distressing.

3. To all, as to the spirit and mighty power of true prayer.

JABEZ BURNS

---

## PRAYER PROMISES

---

They are comprehensive:

   I. Prayer of the righteous availeth much (James 5:16).

  II. Ask and it shall be given (Matt. 7:7-11).

 III. Agree and it shall be done (Matt. 18:19).

 IV. Abide, then ask what ye will (John 15:7).

  V. In My name and I will do (John 14:13,14; 16:23,24).

 VI. Able to do above our asking or thinking (Eph. 3:20).

HENRY W. FROST